WAGGING MY TALES

Douglas Carlson DVM

Copyright © 2021 Douglas Carlson DVM
All rights reserved
First Edition

PAGE PUBLISHING, INC.
Conneaut Lake, PA

First originally published by Page Publishing 2021

ISBN 978-1-6624-6212-2 (pbk)
ISBN 978-1-6624-6214-6 (digital)

Printed in the United States of America

CONTENTS

Acknowledgments 5
Prologue 7
Part 1: My Humble Beginnings 9
   1: I've Been Shot...11
   2: Becoming a Midwife (for Pigs) 17
   3: The Life and Times for a Pet Pig...........................21
   4: Prince versus the Omar Man 26
   5: Becoming a Red-Hot Showman...............................32
Part 2: Achieving My Desire to Become a Veterinarian 37
Part 3: My Experiences and Joys of Being a Veterinarian...............43
   1: Butkus: the Junkyard Dog 45
   2: Unique Patients Call for Unique Treatments.....................48
   3: Surprise, Surprise, Surprise 52
   4: Pepi Is Gone 57
   5: Cats Do Have Nine Lives 60
   6: Stepping Up to Be a Midwife 64
   7: You Can't Judge a Book by Its Cover....................68
   8: Second Chance for Maggie 72
   9: Always Pick Up Your Underwear 76
   10: Go, Cubbie, Go! 80
   11: Omg! What Did You Eat!.....................................83
   12: The San Francisco Treat 86

ACKNOWLEDGMENTS

My special thanks to my wife, Paulette, whose continual loving support encouraged me to tell my stories. Also, my thanks to my dear clients and patients who made it fun and exciting to go to work every day.

Although these stories are actual true events, the names of the clients and patients have been changed to protect their privacy.

PROLOGUE

I was very fortunate to grow up in a loving, close-knit family where we would all help with the work of the farm while enjoying each other's company. We learned the value of hard work. All three of us kids in the family started our formal education in a one-room country school house, where one teacher taught twenty-two kids from first through eighth grade. Yet all three of us received college degrees and had done well with our professional careers.

This book is separated in three parts. The first part is a collection of my personal experiences growing up on the farm, which led me to become a veterinarian. My early life experiences developed my need to care and treat for sick and injured animals and to go the extra mile to do everything possible to help a suffering animal. The second part briefly describes the struggles I had to get into veterinary school. The third part is a collection of stories about some of my unusual patients over my forty-two years of practice.

Because I had developed Parkinson's disease, I have recently retired after treating animals for forty-two years. My daughter, Dr. Amanda Healey, has done a great job in taking over the veterinary practice. My career has been very rewarding as my work has allowed me to fulfill my dream of helping animals. My veterinary practice has been named as one of the top veterinary practices by *Chicago* magazine. However, my best reward was that I always looked forward to going to work at Village Animal Clinic every day to fulfill my childhood dream.

PART 1

My Humble Beginnings

I'VE BEEN SHOT

Spring was an exciting time on the farm in Iowa. The snow was melting, and the days were longer. The grass started turning green, and everything seemed to come to life after a long dark and dreary winter. My brother, Denny; my sister, Janet; and I had a contest on who would spot the first robin because we knew that was the official first day of spring, even though it said on the Farmers Mercantile calendar that the first day of spring was March 21.

However, one of the most exciting first days of spring was the day we went into the town of Red Oak and stopped at the Oakfield Hatchery to buy several hundred baby chicks. The baby chicks were stuffed into three-foot-by-three-foot boxes, which were only six inches high. There were silver dollar-size cutouts around the sides and throughout the lid on top to give them air, but since there were about fifty baby chicks in each box, they didn't have any room to hardly breathe anyway.

I was anxious to get the baby chicks home to give them freedom and be able to enjoy watching them run around the chicken house. Since it was still cold outside, my dad had placed four heat lamps from the ceiling. The chicks soon found the warmth of the lamps. Mom filled the water bottles, which were our one gallon jars inverted upside down into a saucer that allowed a constant level of water for the chicks to drink.

"Mom, can I fill the feeders for the chicks?" I said.

Mom said, "Sure, but don't spill the grain." I cautiously took an old butternut coffee can and dipped it into the fifty-pound bag of feed. I then carefully poured the feed into the trough, which was three feet long and only three inches wide. I was thrilled to see the few-day-old chicks scamper to start eating the finely ground grain.

To keep the chicks from jumping into the feeders, a roller was located over the top of the feeder, and I noticed that as soon as a chick jumped on the roller, it fell off. And they quickly learned to only eat from the side of the feeder. I was amazed on how quickly a small few-day-old chick could learn to eat, find water, and find the warm spots under the heat lamps.

Mom said, "It's time to go to bed, Dougie. You have school tomorrow."

I replied, "Can't I stay and watch the chicks a little longer?"

Mom replied, "The chicks will be here tomorrow, so you can enjoy them then."

I couldn't wait to get home from school the next day. As soon as I got off the bus, I quickly ate one of my mom's sweet rolls and headed straight to the chicken house. I made a quick trip across the cold barnyard and grinned as I opened the door to the chicken house and found hundreds of baby chicks scurrying around under the heat lamps. Even though we had the chicks for only one day, it seemed like they were already growing. I would repeatedly go to the chicken house every day and would watch for the first sign of wing feathers, which only took about one week to grow. Slowly as the weeks would go by, the fuzzy yellow feathers would be totally replaced by white longer feathers.

When the baby chicks reached a certain size, it was time to transfer the chicks to a larger chicken house with a completely attached wired-in outdoor area. The pullets (the female chickens) were put in one side of the house where they had cubicles to lay their eggs. The roosters (the male chickens) were put in another side of the house, and they would be fed to a certain weight until it was time to slaughter and dress them out so we could have our traditional fried chicken every Sunday after church.

Mom and Dad would transfer the chickens by each carrying three chickens by their legs in each hand and walking 300 yards from the baby chicken house to the hen and rooster house. I thought I was a big boy when Dad allowed me to carry one chicken. Even though it was wiggling during the entire walk, I had to hold the chicken out from my legs as I was afraid that the chicken would peck at my legs while walking. I would transfer the chicken from one arm to another to rest my aching arm, and the 300 yards seemed like a mile to me.

One night in the wee hours of the morning, I heard my dad in the next bedroom hollering, "Some foxes are in the henhouse killing the chickens!" Dad was hurriedly putting on his bib overalls, and he ran downstairs, grabbing his shotgun as he headed out the door, not even taking time to put on his coat. As he headed for the henhouse, he saw two red foxes scurrying under the wire fence and carrying dead chickens in their mouths. Dad fired a couple of shots, but they were running too fast and too far away. Upon entering the henhouse, he found four other chickens dead under the roost.

Dad was furious, and he yelled some words in Swedish, which, he always told me, meant "That is terrible." He would often say different phrases in Swedish, but he said that they all meant the same thing: "That is terrible." Two weeks earlier, some foxes got into the farrowing house and killed two baby pigs, which were only a few days old. It seemed that the foxes were getting more aggressive and more populated in our area of southwest Iowa. The winter had been quite cold and snowy, so apparently they were very hungry.

Since my dad was a teenager, one of his passions was hunting. However, I didn't see him go hunting many times as he always seemed busy on the farm. But the problem with the foxes encouraged him to take some action in reducing the fox population. Dad called on some of our neighbors and friends who liked to hunt.

That was the beginning of the Sure-As-Shooting Fox Club. Dad asked his friends and neighbors to spread the word to invite anyone who wanted to help with the fox problem to come to our farm every Monday at noon during the winter months. Dad put a notice in the local newspaper, *the Red Oak Express*, and on the first Monday, they had twenty farmers meet at the farm. Dad planned what sections of land to hunt; usually three or four sections were hunted every Monday. Each section had a starting time where they would divide up around the section, which was one mile on each side. So if there were twenty hunters, five hunters would space themselves evenly on each side and then begin to walk to the center to *round up* the foxes.

On the first Monday, they bagged three foxes, but four got away because they only had twenty hunters.

After the hunt, everyone would meet back at the farm where we had a big coffee urn and rolls to feed the hunters. I thought that was great because as soon as I got off the school bus, I would run into the garage and grab a sweet roll.

The three foxes were hung up on the garage wall, and my dad took a picture of the three foxes and the three hunters who bagged each fox. Dad then submitted the picture and the report of fox club to the *Red Oak Express*. The following Thursday, the picture of the three foxes and three hunters was on the front page of the *Express*. The newly formed fox club was the talk of the town. When we stopped at the coffee shop at JD Oil, as soon as my dad walked in, everyone was saying, "Hey, Paul, tell me about your fox club." After church on Sunday morning, my dad was surrounded by churchmen who wanted to know more about the club. Meanwhile, my mom was anxious to get home and finish our Sunday dinner of fried chicken and mash potatoes.

The next Monday, there were over forty farmers and hunters who showed up on the farm. When I got off the school bus that Monday, our lane from the road up to the house and the yard around the barn and corncrib was filled with pickups. That Monday, the club bagged ten foxes, and only one got away. The more hunters they had, the less likely they were to get away. Dad again hung up the foxes on the garage wall and took another picture with the hunters for the *Red Oak Express*.

The Sure-As-Shooting Fox Club continued to grow, and during their inaugural year, they bagged eighty-four foxes and seven coyotes. After the hunt, my dad would cut off the ears of the foxes and coyotes and bring them into the Red Oak courthouse. The county had a program where they would pay two dollars for each pair of a fox's ears and five dollars for each pair of a coyote's ears. Dad would use this money to help pay for the rolls from the bakery, but there was always money left over. So at the end of the season, Dad would rent the Odd Fellows Hall and put on an "oyster feed." My mom and some of the other farmers' wives would cook oysters stew with all the trimmings.

Already, the men were talking about what sections to hunt next winter, so therefore, a tradition was started at our farm.

I was always excited as a boy for each Monday to arrive, mainly so I could grab a sweet roll after school and listen to the farmers tell their funny stories. One Monday, there was no school because of teachers' meetings. My dad asked me if I would like to walk alongside of him for the Monday afternoon hunt. I was a big fan of Roy Rogers, Hopalong Cassidy, Gabby Hayes, Gene Autry, and others on TV. I also read a lot about Davy Crockett from books I checked out from Ms. Winters at the Red Oak library. To put it mildly, I was really excited to go on the hunt.

Mom helped me get my winter coat, gloves, and five buckle overshoes to be ready for the hunt. It was a sunny twenty-degree day with about four inches of snow on the farmland. Mom had cooked a pork roast for dinner before noon so we wouldn't get hungry, but I was too excited to eat much.

We started walking the first section of the day at our neighbor's farm, which belonged to Harold Gasson. We first had to walk by his beef cows in his pasture. Spring calving had not started yet, so all the cows seemed content as we walked by. We traipsed through the cornfields, which had been picked of their corn. However, it was quite awkward to step over the cornrows stubble. Finally, we got to an alfalfa hayfield, and the walking became easier. We were getting close to the center of the section as I could see some hunters wearing fluorescent caps on the opposite side. I was on my first section, but my legs were already getting tired. But I wouldn't admit it to my dad.

Suddenly, my dad said, "Look to your right." And I spotted a red fox sprinting back and forth on the hayfield. He was becoming quite frantic as he would run one way to get away from the hunters. Then he would see the hunters on the other side and frantically change direction to avoid the other hunters. None of the hunters had fired their shotguns yet as he was still out of range. As we were close to the center of the section, the space between hunters was now only about thirty yards, so the frantic fox could not find an escape route.

Leo Bruce, who was on our right side, fired the first shot. He missed, but it caused the fox to run away from us. When the fox got to the other side, Carroll Pendegraft fired his shotgun, and he, too, missed the fox. I was beginning to hope that the fox would escape as you could see how he was extremely frightened from all the hunters. At this point, the fox started running back to my dad and me. Dad pointed his Winchester Model 12 shotgun and fired away. The fox started rolling over and over and finally stopped moving. I knew I should be happy that my dad shot the fox, but I was actually feeling pretty sad that this fox lost his life.

I didn't see any other foxes get shot the rest of the afternoon, and I was secretly glad about that. Back at the farm, we all enjoyed the sweet rolls, but the hunter's funny stories didn't seem quite so interesting. Dad got his picture taken with the foxes on the garage wall along with the other hunters. I kept looking at the eyes of the dead fox and remembering how frantic he was as he tried to escape from the hunters.

Later that night, I woke up again in the wee hours of the morning. However, this time, it was not about Dad chasing the foxes out of the henhouse. This time, I woke up dreaming I was a fox, and I, too, was surrounded by hunters. A hunter would shoot at me, and I would dart away in the opposite direction. I was frantic, and my heart was pounding. As several hunters would continue to shoot at me, I was starting to think I could get away. I saw a gap in the hunters where there was some tall weeds, and I thought I could sneak away.

About that time, I heard a big bang and found myself rolling over and over again. I then realized I had been shot. I jumped out of bed and ran into my parents' bedroom frantically screaming, "I've been shot. I've been shot!" My parents sat up in bed suddenly with bewildered looks on their faces. They turned on the light, and I then realized I was not actually a fox and that I had a bad dream. I finally fell back to sleep after crawling into the security of my parents' bed.

From that night forward, I didn't look forward to Mondays quite so much, except for the sweet rolls.

BECOMING A MIDWIFE (FOR PIGS)

When I was eight years old, my dad decided to raise purebred Hampshire hogs. Dad had raised pigs before for market, but now he decided he wanted to raise purebreds to be sold for breeding stock rather than being sent to market. We started going to different auctions of purebred Hampshire hogs to build a stock of good breeding hogs.

It was always fun to travel with Dad to the auctions. I liked spending the time with Dad and I really enjoyed the excitement of the auctioneer trying to get the highest bid for the hogs. After several auctions, Dad bought his first boar called Mr. Iowa. He had been the first place finisher at the Iowa State Fair, and Dad thought that even though he paid a lot of money for Mr. Iowa, it was the quickest and best way to quickly develop some good breeding stock.

As the years went by, Dad became well-known for his quality breeding stock. Every winter, we would have boar and gilt sales at our farm. Dad put up a Quonset building where it was designed to have a sale ring and holding pens for the auction. The sale would be advertised all across the state of Iowa, and it was customary to provide a dinner for the guests before the sale. Mom would work hard to set up ham sandwiches (of course) and potato salad for all the guests coming to the farm for the sale. On the day of the sale, our farm was filled with 150 vehicles and 250 people attending the sale. The auctioneer was hired, who was well-known in the purebred Hampshire hog business, and he knew how to work the crowd to get the best price for each boar and gilt.

As Dad's purebred hog business increased, he also increased the number of hogs he raised to keep up with the demand. At one point, he had one hundred sows farrowing and delivering baby pigs twice a year. Based on those numbers, with an average of eight pigs per litter, Dad was producing 1,600 pigs per year, and we averaged four sows having baby pigs every week. Dad spent a lot of sleepless nights watching and helping sows farrow their baby pigs. Oftentimes, the local veterinarian made visits to the farm to help pull the baby pigs during farrowing or possibly do a Cesarean. Because I was still a small boy of ten years, Dad would often ask me to help deliver the baby pigs. My arm and hand was small, so I could often help out a sow who was having trouble delivering her pigs. I would "lube up" and reach into the vaginal canal and pull the baby pig out, who was stuck in the birth canal. This not only prevented the sow from having a Cesarean but also it improved the odds of delivering live baby pigs. For me, it was a great feeling to be able to deliver a baby pig alive, rather than see it die. I was always excited even if it was late into the night. There was no greater feeling than being able to bring a live animal into this world who otherwise might have died.

To help promote Dad's purebred Hampshire hogs, we routinely showed our pigs at the Iowa State Fair. I loved the fair and enjoyed all the festivities that the fair provided. My brother, Denny, and I would initially start showing our 4-H hogs at the fair for the first three days. Then Dad and the other purebred hog breeders from around the Midwest would show and exhibit their hogs for the next seven days. As a result, I would be at the fair for the full ten days.

Because the hogs were required to be at the fair for the whole ten days, Dad would need to go back home after the shows to take care of things on the farm. He would have my brother and I stay at the fair and take care of the hogs so he could get back to the farm. We would stay in the 4-H building and be responsible for Dad's show hogs. It didn't take long to take care of the pigs, and we had a lot of time to hang around the fair and see all the exhibits and the midway.

In 1960 when I had just turned fourteen years old, Dad asked me to stay and take care of his show hogs by myself for five days. My brother, Denny, was now sixteen, and he had to help on the farm. I was somewhat nervous about staying at the fair by myself but agreed as I had felt comfortable with my brother during the previous years. Dad had exhibited twelve hogs that year, but one of the hogs was shown in a Bred Sow class. And she was due to farrow two days after the fair was over. Everything went well for the first three days. I would get up early and feed the pigs, clean the pens, and then walk around the fair and enjoy some great food. I thought I was doing pretty well. But on the fourth day, the pregnant sow came down with milk, and she stopped eating. I knew she was getting ready to deliver her baby pigs.

As the day went along, she became very quiet and seemed content to only lie in her pen and not move. I knew she was having contractions, but there was no sign of any "pigging." I walked over to the veterinarian's office and told him of the situation. He came by and gave the sow an injection of oxytocin to stimulate uterine contractions. He then told me to call him if the sow didn't start pigging. Nothing happened for one hour. Then the sow developed some strong contractions but no sight of any baby pigs.

I knew she was in trouble and thought she may need a Cesarean. So, at this point, I decided to lube up and *see what I could do*. I reached my small hand and arm into the vaginal canal and found the baby pig was coming breech (tail first). I could barely feel the tail, but during one of the contractions, the pig was thrust enough for me to get my hand around its pelvis. I then was able to pull the baby pig out, and to my surprise, it was alive. I was ecstatic. After the breech delivery, the remaining six pigs were delivered normally without any distress. All the pigs looked healthy, and they were all nursing from the sow.

At midnight, I was satisfied that all the pigs were doing well, so I went back to the 4-H dorm as I was exhausted. I was up at 6:00 a.m. to check on the sow and baby pigs. All was well, and the pigs were all nursing. And the sow was grunting with content. I went back to the 4-H dorm for a much-needed breakfast.

When I returned to the swine barn after breakfast, I found approximately twenty people standing around the pen where the sow had her pigs. I was really worried something had happened. But as I approached the pen, the people were admiring the sow and the new litter of pigs. I suddenly found myself grinning from ear to ear. They all started asking me questions about the newborn pigs, and I was more than happy to provide all the details. I did not venture off this day to buy a foot-long hot dog on a stick or off to get a Bob's lemonade. Instead, I spent the entire day at the swine barn enjoying all the attention that our newborn pigs were providing all the fairgoers.

The fair veterinarian came by later that morning and looked at the sow and gave her another injection of oxytocin. I could still remember his words: "Good job, son." I'm still grinning from ear to ear.

THE LIFE AND TIMES FOR A PET PIG

As the years went by, my dad became more involved in raising purebred Hampshire hogs. We would enter our prized pigs to many fairs, and it became more important to my dad to win the top prize at the shows.

Because my dad wanted to do everything possible to breed a top-quality pig, we went to many hog shows and sales to find that perfect boar or gilt to improve the quality of our herd. One of the many shows and sales that we attended was a trip to Madison, Wisconsin, as Dad had heard many top-quality hogs would be available for sale. From Red Oak, Iowa, to Madison, Wisconsin, it was a good nine-hour drive. Because we were busy on the farm with the normal farming obligations of cultivating the corn and putting up the hay, Dad decided to make the trip to Madison and back home all in one day.

So we left at 3:00 a.m. to arrive in Madison at noon. I was nervous about being ready at 3:00 a.m. for our big trip, so I came up with a great way to be ready to go with Dad in the middle of the night. Being resourceful, I went ahead and put on the clothes I was planning to wear on the trip and then simply put my pajamas on top of my clothes to crawl into bed. Mom came to tuck me into bed and noticed the extra layer of clothes, and she laughed and laughed. So I gave up my novel "get ready quick" idea and only wore my pajamas.

Mom woke me up at 3: a.m. and gave us a bag of snacks, and we were out the door and into the red International pickup for our nine-hour journey. I took two really great naps as we finally made our way to Madison by noon. We watched the hog show, and Dad carefully selected a boar who he thought would help his breeding program. After the show, an auction began around 8:00 p.m. for a chance to buy the prized pigs. I always loved the auctions as the auctioneers were quite colorful in their approach to keep the bidding active and get the best price. When I was alone, I would often try to mimic the auctioneers and make up my own colorful expressions to be entertaining.

When Dad's selected boar walked into the sale ring, I was nervous that Dad would not be able to get the boar for the price he was willing to pay and all our efforts would be for nothing. One of the auctioneers' name was Pig Paul, and he kept watching my dad closely as the bidding process began. Every time Dad would raise the bid, Pig Paul would holler out a very loud and long "Yeeeeeeeep!" Finally, the other bidders stopped, and my dad happily landed his prized boar.

So we loaded up our new addition in our red International pickup and headed for Red Oak, Iowa. The only problem was that it was now 11:00 p.m. I could tell that Dad was tired, but he said it was okay for me to sleep. Around 4:00 a.m., I woke up hearing my dad singing. My dad had a lot of great qualities, but singing was definitely not one of those. When I would stand next to my dad singing hymns in church, I would be embarrassed of the awful sounds coming out of my dad's mouth. So his singing definitely woke me up, and I started laughing. Fortunately, my laughing and Dad's singing gave him a burst of energy and kept him wide awake. The next three hours, we both sang and laughed until we arrived home. That was the only time that Dad and I sang together, and even though the singing was horrible, we both enjoyed our songfest.

The new boar worked out well, and Dad's reputation as one who raised top-quality Hampshire hogs continued to increase.

Because we had many visitors to the farm to buy breeding stock, it was very important that the farm and all the farm buildings and fences be in top condition. Every summer, my brother, Denny, and I would spend a lot of our time painting the white board fences and keeping the grass mowed so everything looked pristine for our visitors.

When someone would visit the farm to look at the pigs, my dad would insist they wear rubber boots and clean coveralls so disease would not be brought into the herd. This also gave the impression to the potential hog buyer that a lot of effort went into raising top-quality, disease-free hogs.

One salesmanship tactic that bothered me at the time was how my dad handled a runt pig. A runt pig was small and poorly developed when it was born, and it never seemed to catch up with the rest of the litter. It might have many different causes for it being a runt, such as an underdeveloped liver or intestinal tract. The bottom line was that they never developed and often would die at a few weeks of age. They did not give a favorable impression to the potential hog buyer, and economically, they were a liability. So the solution was for my dad to grasp the piglet and lie it down on the concrete and then simply smash the head with a ball-peen hammer. The piglet would suddenly become lifeless without a struggle, and the remains would be thrown into the manure pile. I would often look away as the piglet quickly lost his life. I later realized that this method was very humane as it caused sudden death similar to how animals were slaughtered at packing plants.

However, one summer day, the picture book appearance of my dad's pristine hog farm became disrupted. Out of the blue, a thirty-pound white pig came walking up our driveway. This pig definitely looked out of place in the midst of multiple hog lots of homogeneous Hampshire hogs with their characteristic white belts around their shoulders and front legs next to their black bodies. This pig was amazingly friendly and wanted to be petted immediately. I ran and fetched some water and fed for this new arrival, and I suddenly became bonded to this new "out of place" creature.

We often had stray dogs dropped off on our farm, and occasionally, our neighbors' cows would get out and make it to our barnyard. But this was the only time a stray pig showed up in our barnyard. Dad wasn't too excited about this new arrival because he worried about this newcomer bringing in disease, and certainly, the appearance of this pig did not look good to our farm visitors. So even though our nearest farm place was over a mile away, Dad thought he could find the rightful owner of this out-of-place pig. Dad immediately called neighbors Levi, Ivan, Clark, Carroll, and Vernon, and none of them had a pig fitting his description.

In the meantime, I had now named the pig "Whitey," and I continued to pet him by rubbing his neck behind his ears and scratching his belly. He would follow me around the barnyard, but I was careful not to let him get close to any of Dad's purebred pigs. I knew Dad would never allow this pig to mingle with his prized pigs, but I knew I would have a tough time to convince my dad to keep the stray.

As a young boy, I saw my dad being tough and strong. I saw him throw 100-pound hay bales over his head in 100-degree heat for several hours in a row. I saw him wake up at 4:00 a.m. and work until 10:00 p.m. being totally exhausted but never complaining. Once, when we were shelling corn out of the corncrib, my dad was scooping the remains of the ear of corn into the sheller. Suddenly, from the small pile of remaining corn, a big gray rat came running out. I immediately started scaling up the side of the corncrib like a monkey. Then to my shock, the rat seemed like it had no place to go, so it suddenly ran up the pant leg of my dad's OshKosh B'gosh overalls.

I could see the rat struggling through the pants when my dad calmly reached for his pliers, which he kept in a holster on his belt, and squeezed the neck of the rat until it went limp. The rat then fell onto the floor of the crib, lifeless. My eyes were as big as silver dollars, and I was sure I was white as a sheet. When I regained my composure, I escaped the corncrib, while Dad finished the task of scooping the last remains of the corn. My TV heroes, such as Roy Rogers, Gene Autry, and Hopalong Cassidy, never showed as much bravery and courage as my dad did on that day.

So how was I going to convince my tough and strong dad to take in this helpless thirty-pound pig? I remembered that Dad had a small empty grain bin in one side of the boxcar. It was about eight feet square with no windows and no ventilation. The oats had already been combined, so I knew Dad would not need the space until next year. So I begged Dad for me to keep Whitey in the grain bin. I would feed and water Whitey twice daily and take him for walks around the barnyard and never let him associate with any of the purebred-prized pigs. I was sure my dad had been watching me play with Whitey and realized that my dad had a soft spot for animals. He gave me a smile and didn't hesitate to let me keep Whitey.

I spent the rest of the summer taking special care of Whitey. He would follow me around the barnyard, and his favorite thing was for me to rub his belly. He was truly like a pet dog, and he was always excited to see me. If our world did not have cats and dogs for us to enjoy in our homes, I was sure we would have pet pigs as they were friendly, had good temperaments, were clean, and were easily house trained.

As we got into the fall, Whitey had now grown from 35 pounds to 180 pounds. He was still my pet pig, but he was not as playful as before. He was now "market weight." All of the other pigs on the farm were either kept for breeding or sent to the market when they reached 180 pounds. So my mom and dad sat down with me at the kitchen table and said Whitey needed to go to market. I got a lump in my throat, and I bit my lip to hold back my tears. But I merely said okay and nothing else. For the first time on the farm, Whitey got to mingle with the other Hampshire-prized pigs as I watched him being loaded up on the truck. Whitey was always such a happy pig, and he seemed happy to be around with pigs like himself. He certainly was unaware of his fate.

For the months following, my pork-chop dinners and pork roasts didn't quite taste the same.

PRINCE VERSUS THE OMAR MAN

Besides Whitey, the pet pig, we had other pets that inhabited our farm. We were well-supplied with cats, dogs, and even a pet pheasant.

Most farms had cats and dogs, but we were quite unique in that we had a pet rooster pheasant named Pretty Boy. In the mid-1950s, the local Izaak Walton League determined that there was a shortage of pheasants in southwest Iowa. Therefore, many of the local farmers were asked to take newly hatched pheasants and raise them to maturity like we did for our chickens. Then they would be set free in strategic areas in southwest Iowa to replenish the pheasant supply.

My dad took in 200 baby pheasants and nurtured them to maturity so they could be released into the wild. Dad would then take them to the designated areas for release. However, Dad decided to release a handful of pheasants around the farm. To our surprise, one of the rooster pheasants decided to stay around the barnyard rather than venture off to the cornfields and protected areas in the fields. I guess he decided that the room and board at the barnyard was much better than fending for oneself in the fields. Pretty Boy became very friendly and was not scared to be around people. In fact, my brother, Denny, and I would tease Pretty Boy by flipping our baseball caps under his beak. He would fly three feet up in the air and make spurring motions with his feet. We would then start running, and Pretty Boy would chase after us boys. Fortunately, he never pecked our legs, but I was always somewhat fearful he would catch us. Dad took an 8-mm home movie of Pretty Boy and sent it to WOW TV in Omaha, who quickly put it on their ten o'clock news.

As summer came to an end and pheasant season opened in the fall in Iowa, Pretty Boy no longer showed up around the barnyard. I was sure a pheasant hunter came through our farm and found this crazy pheasant that ran toward the hunter rather than running or flying away. The hunter probably told this unbelievable story to all the locals at the JD Café.

Cats were also quite numerous on the Carlson farm, but they were not friendly as they never were given people contact to help them develop trust in human beings. There were often ten to fifteen adult cats roaming around the farm. Mom would put out table scraps for the cats, and they also survived by showing up when it was time to milk the cows. Dad would always put some of the fresh raw milk in a pan when he was milking, and I enjoyed watching all the cats frantically dive into the milk like it was their last meal.

I tried repeatedly to catch one of the cats or young kittens. But they would only allow me to get within a few feet before running away because they never developed trust in the human touch. I knew that if I would find a newborn litter of kittens when they were born, I could possibly *tame* one of the kittens and develop it into a loving, friendly cat.

I was constantly on the lookout for one of the hiding places that a mother cat would hide her kittens. The mother cats were very resourceful and always seemed to find really good hiding places. However, one day when I was in the Quonset building where Dad stored machinery and had our hog sales, I spotted a gray tabby mother cat sneak behind the hay mower. I purposely did not look for the kittens at that time when the mother cat was present. Instead, I went back to the hay mower later in the day and crawled behind the hay mower and rake. I then found a nest of kittens snuggled under the hay rake.

I was able to pick them up, and I used my work gloves to pet them so my human scent would not be left on them. They were only 7–10 days old as their eyes were just starting to open. I repeated my visits to the kittens at least once daily, and they were becoming quite comfortable with my handling and petting. If the mother cat was around, I would not approach the kittens as I didn't want the mother cat to move them if she suspected I was petting her kittens. Otherwise, I knew the mother would relocate the kids to another hiding location.

As the weeks went by, they became more playful and always happy to see me when I made my visits. I was glad that we would at least have some farm cats that could be picked up and handled. I would bring them some food and cow's milk. As the kittens continued to grow, they became more trusting of my presence and would start running toward me as soon as I entered the Quonset building. They also started to explore around the barnyard, and I was glad they were able to find the barn where Dad milked the cows. They were excited and anxious to join in the fracas to get some of the fresh cow's milk along with the other resident cats of the farm.

One day during the evening milking of the cows, I noticed one of the kittens did not seem anxious to join in for the pan of cow's milk. The next day, I saw only one of the kittens going for the milk pan. The other kittens seemed to have disappeared. I began to search the farm for the three kittens and looked at every potential hiding spot. After several days, I found one of the kittens dead in a ditch in the pasture. His eyes and nostrils were filled with mucous, and he seemed very thin.

Apparently, the kittens had picked up a respiratory virus and died within a few days. Because all of the resident cats were wild and unable to be caught, they were not vaccinated although my dad probably would not have spent the money for "just a cat" to be vaccinated. I also noticed there were less resident cats showing up for the milking. The virus had reduced the population of our cats, and only those who had street virus antibodies in their system were able to survive. I was very disappointed that the special group of kittens that I domesticated fell victims to the nasty respiratory virus. Sometimes the *survival of the fittest* was not fair in Mother Nature.

Almost all farmers would have a farm dog, and they were called working dogs rather than pets. Many farmers had collies to help with the herding of cattle and pigs.

My dad always enjoyed the smaller feisty-type dogs. He always had a liking for rat terriers as he hoped they would help reduce the rat population on the farm. So one day, Dad came home with a rat terrier, which actually was a purebred Manchester terrier. She was promptly named Poochie, and she quickly became embraced by our family. However, the life of a farm dog was quite different from today's pampered pet dogs. It was considered taboo to keep your farm dog in the house even though everyone in the family would be devastated if anything happened to Poochie. Her job was to patrol the farm for mice and rats and not be pampered by the good life.

Poochie did graduate to the privilege of staying out on the back porch of our house at night. I would also sneak Poochie into the house in the afternoon and liked to take my afternoon nap with Poochie sleeping in my arms. I considered Poochie to be the perfect dog, and she loved all the attention of our family.

Dad also felt Poochie was a great dog, and therefore, she should be bred to raise puppies. So Dad found a Manchester terrier breeder in Henderson who had a top-quality, stylish male dog to sell. He was four months old and very energetic. Because of his stylish characteristics, he was named Prince. As Prince became mature, we noticed that Prince was much more feisty than Poochie and not as friendly. If any neighbor or feed salesman would visit the farm, he would bark ferociously and act like he was going to tear them apart. Fortunately, Prince never bit anyone, but his menacing bark and manner kept rookie visitors to the farm from getting out of their car until we took control of Prince.

Later that summer, Dad noticed that Poochie was pregnant and developing a "pouch" of her unborn puppies. Poochie was able to stay in the house more often at this time although she always was put out on the porch at bedtime. One morning as I came down for breakfast, Mom and Dad were smiling, and they gave me the exiting news that Poochie had four puppies. I quickly ran out onto the porch and found four little fuzzy pups snuggled under Poochie's belly. Poochie looked very content as she nestled her pups close to her.

It was exciting to watch the pups grow and develop. They opened their eyes at ten days, and by three weeks of age, they were running around the porch and exploring what they could get into. When they were eight weeks of age, they were ready to be sold and placed in a new home. I did not look forward to the day when I had to say goodbye to one of the pups.

One summer night as it was getting dark, we noticed that one of the pups was not coming up to the house for their evening feeding. The pup that was gone was Dusty, and he was probably the most feisty pup, similar in temperament to his father, Prince. So all five of our family—my mom; my dad; my sister, Janet; and my brother, Denny—started a search patrol for Dusty. We all looked around the barnyard and checked all the crooks and crannies of the farm buildings, constantly yelling for Dusty to respond. To our disappointment, no trace of Dusty could be found. We then noticed that Poochie was whining and starting to run toward our neighbor's cornfield. So we redirected our search to the cornfield. As it was getting dark, we were becoming more worried about finding Dusty. We again split up and started walking through the cornfield. Earlier in the summer, I had stepped on a bull snake as I was walking through the cornfield cutting out cockleburs. So I was not too comfortable walking through a cornfield as it was getting dark.

Suddenly, I heard a faint whimper of a puppy, and I quickly noticed little Dusty huddled up at the base of the cornstalks. I called his name, and he perked up and came running toward me. I don't know who was happier, Dusty or myself, as I picked him up and cradled him in my arms while I was yelling to the other family members that Dusty was found.

Within the next few weeks, I had to say goodbye to the pups as they were placed in their new homes. The departure of Dusty was especially difficult as he had a special place in my heart.

Our farm was mostly self-sufficient to provide food for our family. We would butcher one of our hogs, raise chickens, grow vegetables from our garden, and save milk from our cows to provide nearly all the food our family would require. However, one of our luxuries was the delivery of fresh bread from the "Omar man." The Omar man had a route, and he would deliver many different types of bread on a weekly basis. My favorite was their raisin bread.

Even though he was a regular visitor to our farm, Prince would go crazy every time the Omar man delivered his bread. He would bark and chase him ferociously as he arrived at the farm. I was sure that the Omar man was not pleased with Prince. One morning as the Omar man was leaving, Prince again chased after him as he was driving down the lane. Suddenly, we heard a squeal and rushed outside to find that Prince had been run over by the truck tire. By the time we got to Prince, he laid lifeless on the driveway. Dad was mad at the Omar man, but he was very apologetic and said he could not avoid hitting him.

So in only a few weeks, we went from six dogs to one. The barnyard did not seem the same anymore with Prince and the pups roaming around. We decided to cancel the delivery of our bread from the Omar man. Not being able to eat my raisin bread was a small consolation for the loss of Prince.

BECOMING A RED-HOT SHOWMAN

<<insert image here>>

Saturday nights were exciting in our small Iowa town of Red Oak. Like many small towns in Iowa, the center of the town was the city square. The center square consisted of an open park with retail stores and restaurants around the periphery of the park. A large eight-foot water fountain built with large rocks was located in the very center of the square. We would like the challenge of climbing to the top of the water fountain and yell, "King of the Mountain!" If we would see one of the two town cops while climbing, we would scurry down and run for the alley to avoid a lecture. The men playing checkers on the nearby tables would always get a chuckle as we would scamper off.

Saturday nights were special. That was the only night when the stores were open. It became a tradition to spend your Saturday nights on the square, meeting up with friends and going into the various stores. There was a wide variety of stores that attracted many shoppers on a Saturday night. Western Auto store was located on the northwest corner, and one could buy your fuzzy dice and other accessories for your car. Schoenberg's offered ladies dresses and apparel. Houghton State Bank was on the southwest corner of the square, and that was where my dad helped me open my first savings account where I was able to save to get my balance to ten dollars.

My mom would always take me to the Buster Brown shoe store for new shoes. I always enjoyed trying on the different shoes and then inserting my feet into the fluoroscope machine and see how my toes would fit inside the shoes. And then there was the Green Parrot Café. It had the best fountain drinks and sandwiches. Their french fries were the best. My favorite fountain drink was the Green River although the Sarsaparilla was a close second. Tom, the owner, always took good care of us, but he usually managed to yell at us for something in his Greek accent. Since we could barely understand what he was saying, we didn't pay much attention though.

As a high school student, my favorite establishment was Baldies Pool Hall. It was located under the Iowana theater, which Baldie managed as well. To enter the pool hall, one would go down some old dilapidated stairs into the dingy basement. You were greeted by the aroma of stale smoke and beer. You would look over to your right as you entered the basement and see Lumpy standing behind the bar smoking a cigarette. He always had a big gallon jar of hot pickles sitting on the bar counter. As you would walk across the sticky concrete floor, you would find four snooker tables and four eight ball tables. One of the patrons would then yell to Socks, "Rack them up, Socks," and you would soon hear the sound of someone breaking the rack of balls to start their game. It was quite a seedy place, but it was heaven to us.

Baldie would often collect the admission for the theater above the pool hall as well. My wife, Paulette, told of the time when she was nine years old that she and her friend, Steve Johnson, were given twenty cents each to go to the Saturday afternoon matinee. Steve would walk along with Paulette for six blocks to the theater. Upon arrival, Steve gave his two dimes to Baldie. Paulette then reached into her cute little purse for her dimes. Unfortunately, she could only find one dime. Either one of the dimes fell out or it was lodged into the folds of the purse somewhere. Paulette gave Baldie one dime, and Baldie kept looking at Paulette with his evil eye and hoping his intimidation would bring him the other dime. Paulette was motionless and could not say anything. After a period of awkward silence, Baldie finally looked at Steve and then at Paulette again and said, "Okay, go on in." From that point on, Paulette always made sure she had enough money.

However, the store which I liked the most was Kolterman's variety store. Why? You could buy items ranging from kitchen utensils, cookware, towels, various soaps, to cleaning items. However, my eyes would light up when I saw the huge candy counter. The candy counter consisted of huge glass receptacles containing a multitude of different candies. You could choose your favorite candy and order your selection not by weight but by the amount of money you had to spend. For example, instead of ordering a pound of chocolate-covered peanuts, which were forty-nine cents per pound, you could merely ask for *ten cents worth*. Since my parents would only allow each of us ten cents to spend on candy, this method became our standard way of buying candy on Saturday night.

I would often buy chocolate-covered peanuts with my ten cents. However, even at forty-nine cents per pound, one would only receive eight pieces of candy. Certainly, that did not seem to be enough to sustain me for the whole week. So I became candy savvy. I would buy red-hot candies because they were small and lightweight. Then I could bring home a big bag of candy for my week ahead.

Our summer days as a family focused on getting our 4-H animals ready for the county fair. The county fair was held on the second week of August, and it was the highlight of summer before we started back to school after Labor Day. All work on the farm came to a halt during those three days at the fair. On fair days, we would get up early to take care of our animals at the fair and not leave until late at night after the conclusion of the performance.

My brother, Denny; my sister, Janet; and I all had young calves to show at the fair. Our dad would take pride in having quality animals for the county fair. Therefore, Dad would arrange for us to buy our calves from Lomas farms where they raised quality Shorthorn cattle. We would travel to the farm in Dad's pick up in May and select the 300-pound calves with the hopes of finding a winner for the county fair.

The next step was to pay Mr. Lomas for your calf. Mr. Malcolm Lomas was also the owner of the Thos. D. Murphy calendar factory in Red Oak. It was famed for being the world's largest calendar factory and was one of the larger employers in the town of Red Oak. Mr. Lomas took pride in his Shorthorn cattle and really enjoyed supporting the young 4-H kids with their calves. His one requirement was to ask the young 4-H kids to come to his house after purchasing their calves. His house was up "on the hill" in Red Oak and one of the larger homes in Red Oak. Coming from a small farmhouse in the country, it seemed as big as a castle. I was always nervous in walking in the parlor of the house and being escorted into the office where Mr. Lomas was sitting. He was always smiling to see us and made us feel quite at home even though I was quite intimidated.

The next step with our 4-H calves was to break them to lead for the show at the county fair. Many of our calves were quite stubborn, and they would plant all four feet into the ground and refuse to budge. We often had to attach our halter leads to our old F-20 tractor and pull them around the barnyard to "break them to lead." One of our Shorthorn calves was extremely obstinate. He would dig into the ground with all four feet and even was able to break the lead pulling from the tractor. Dad then put together a hay rope-type halter so it would not break. This steer would then bolt around the rear tire of the tractor, trying to get away from being pulled. Then he would run around the opposite side of the tractor to the opposite wheel. I was beginning to think this steer would not be able to be shown. However, after multiple trips around the barnyard, perseverance finally paid off, and the young steer gave in to the lead and was ready for the county fair.

Since my dad raised purebred Hampshire hogs, it was very important for my brother and me to do well showing pigs at the county fair. He would select the very best gilt and boar for our 4-H pigs. We would monitor their development closely and provide them with the best of feed. They were also handled frequently and bathed so they would be ready for the show at the fair. As a result, my brother, Denny, or I would typically have the Grand Champion Pig at the fair.

After the conclusion of selecting the Grand Champion Pig, the final event of the Swine Show was the competition for the "Best Showman." This competition did not judge the quality of the pig but instead judged the ability of the person to show the pig in front of the judge. To be a good showman, you need to be able to present your pig to the judge and walk your pig slowly in front of the judge. You needed to keep your eyes on the judge, and as the judge walked away, one needed to follow the path of the judge to continually present your pig in front of the judge.

My brother, Denny, was the usual winner as he had the ability to control his pigs quite well in front of the judge. When I was thirteen, I had a pig that would stay in front of the judge as long as he was stationery. But when the judge walked away, my pig would not want to move, and I would lose contact with the judge. During the previous competition of showing, I became very frustrated with my pig. Hence, I named him Pokey.

So during the best showman competition, I started having the same problem with Pokey, and I could not get him to move. I would pinch him and push him along, but Pokey stayed true to his form and didn't see the need to walk around chasing a judge. I realized I needed to get Pokey moving somehow. So I remembered I had some red-hot candy in my pocket from Kolterman's variety store. I nonchalantly reached into my jeans pocket and pulled out 2–3 pieces and placed them into the rectum of Pokey. That got his attention, and he perked up and started moving frisky around the show ring. For the next ten minutes, I had Pokey in front of the judge at all times. The judge then selected me as the Best Swine Showman. I received a ribbon awarding me as the Best Swine Showman, but I became known as the Red-Hot Showman.

PART 2

Achieving My Desire to Become a Veterinarian

I knew it was tough to get into veterinary school, but nevertheless, I knew that was what I wanted to do for my lifetime career. Currently, the selection process for veterinary school applicants is even more stringent. For my sophomore year in high school English, Mrs. Houseman required us to do a report on what career you had chosen. So naturally, I did my report on being a veterinarian. I soon learned how important it was to not only have good grades but also be well rounded and show leadership skills. I learned that the selection process to veterinary school was very tough and required passing an interview as well as having a minimum grade point average.

Everyone at that time said I was a quiet, shy-type of boy. I knew that I had to overcome that personality type to become a successful veterinarian. I joined my local 4-H club and eventually became president of the club. The Montgomery County 4-H Club also selected me as president. I also joined Hi-Y, which was a service club in high school, and became their president as well.

When it was time to select a college, Iowa State University seemed a logical choice since both my older brother and sister went there. I started my college career in agricultural engineering. I chose that major because our high school counselor said I was good in math and science, which were important to study engineering. Being naive, I didn't really know what an engineer actually did. But off to Iowa State I went.

When I got to Iowa State, I was overwhelmed. The college professors actually expected you to study and not just listen to the teacher and spit out the answers on a test like I did in high school. I found myself two weeks behind in my courses and only had one week of class. My introductory engineering class was particularly mind-boggling. We had to learn the basics of what they called a slide rule. I realized that engineers sat at desks and used their slide rules day after day. I knew that I wouldn't be happy doing that the rest of my life.

So I decided to go to the college admissions office and change my major. They wanted me to take an aptitude test, which I did. This test showed that I liked working with animals and people. So I changed my major to animal science. I finished out my scheduled courses and got Cs in all my courses. I knew that was a far cry from the As that I needed to get into veterinary school.

The next decision was what to do with a BS degree in animal science. My brother was on track to become a buyer for Hormel as he was on the Iowa State meats judging team. However, that did not interest me to spend my days in meat-packing plants. Plus I didn't have the skills that my brother had in meat judging. I knew I could go back to Red Oak and help my dad farm, but for some reason, that did not excite me. So during my sophomore year and only having a 2.6 grade average out of 4, I decided to join the Air Force ROTC program and became flight qualified. In the summer after my sophomore year, I went to ROTC summer camp to catch up with the other Air Force cadets that had been members since their freshmen year.

I came back pumped up after summer camp to be an officer and a pilot in the Air Force. However, at this time, the sentiment of the Vietnam War was changing. I remember taking a class in ROTC where the instructor said, "A lot of people criticize the Vietnam War, but it's the only war we have." I couldn't accept the mentality of this war and knew in less than two years, I would be sent to Vietnam to fly choppers.

It was now the fall quarter of my junior year in school. My grade point had improved to 2.9. I really wanted now more than ever to get to veterinary school, but I knew I would need to improve my grade point to at least a 3.4. I thought if I could get mostly As during my junior year, I would have a chance. So my career paths would be to start veterinary school the next year or go to Vietnam and fly choppers. I did everything possible to improve my chances. I became president of my fraternity. I was accepted to the Alpha Zeta agricultural honorary and became their president. I also served as the publicity chairman of the Block and Bridle Horse Show, which was a prestigious horse show in Des Moines.

I had two courses during my third year that really were important to ace. They were organic chemistry courses that were considered the deal breakers for acceptance into veterinary school. Organic chemistry required that one needed to be able to memorize and retain complex cycles. The veterinary selection committee used those courses to predict how someone would do in veterinary school. At that time, Jud Isebrands, one of my fraternity brothers from my hometown of Red Oak, Iowa, was in graduate school, and he was required to take the same organic chemistry courses. So we studied together every night, and as a result, we both aced the toughest course to help get my acceptance into veterinary school.

There was only seventy-five slots for the incoming first year class in veterinary school. Sixty acceptance letters had gone out in April, but I only received a letter saying I was on the waiting list for the following fifteen positions. I was sweating bullets, but finally my acceptance letter came on June 15. And I was able to start my veterinary career in two months.

PART 3

My Experiences and Joys of Being a Veterinarian

The stories are a reflection of my actual experiences although the names of the pets and their owners along with some of the details have been changed to protect their privacy.

1. Butkus: the Junkyard Dog
2. Unique Patients Call for Unique Treatments
3. Surprise, Surprise, Surprise
4. Pepi Is Gone
5. Cats Do Have Nine Lives
6. Stepping Up to Be a Midwife
7. You Can't Judge a Book by Its Cover
8. Second Chance for Maggie
9. Always Pick Up Your Underwear
10. Go, Cubbie, Go!
11. OMG! What Did You Eat!
12. The San Francisco Treat

BUTKUS: THE JUNKYARD DOG

Butkus was your typical junkyard dog. He was a large ninety-pound mixed breed. My best estimate was that he was a cross between a Doberman, a German shepherd, and a bloodhound. His coat was black and scruffy-looking with mats of fur well embedded into the coat. He had callous elbows and hocks that were the size of silver dollars. His legs were scarred, and his toe pads were as tough as shoe leather.

He lived up to his namesake, Dick Butkus, who played for the Chicago Bears and was considered one of the most feared and intimidating linebackers of his time. My first introduction to Butkus was when he was two years old, and it was Butkus's first introduction to a veterinarian. His owner was Butch, who operated a car repair business. Butkus had the responsibility to protect the car shop when it was closed. I am sure he didn't allow anyone on the premises as his bark and demeanor would scare anyone from attempting to enter the car shop. When Butch made the appointment, the receptionist informed him of the clinic policy that every dog should be on a leash or carried. Since Butkus had never been on a leash in his life, Butch grabbed a log chain and looped it around his neck as he entered the clinic. I expect the other clients in the clinic were maybe a bit concerned as they saw this large dog with a large log chain wrapped around his neck, walking into the clinic. However, Butkus walked into the clinic and totally ignored the other clients and pets. But he certainly grabbed the attention of everyone else.

Butkus was brought to the clinic for vomiting. The previous night as he was guarding the repair shop, Butkus was exposed to gasoline that had been dripping from one of the cars. I was not sure if he laid in the gasoline or licked his fur, which was contaminated with gasoline, but he certainly absorbed enough gasoline to make him sick. I admit that I was intimidated by Butkus as well. I knew his mission in life was to scare off people at the shop, and I was not sure how he would react to my exam and treatment. Butch reassured me that Butkus would be fine. However, I had had many clients tell me that before, and I would end up with an unexpected dog bite. However, as I slowly approached Butkus and started to rub the fur behind his ears, he seemed to relax and enjoy the attention I was giving him. He was an ideal patient and was very cooperative to exam and treat. As he was mildly dehydrated and was suffering from moderate gastritis, I hospitalized him for the day for IV fluids and injectable antibiotics. Butch came back later that day to pick up Butkus. I briefly explained what treatment had been done and encouraged Butch to bring back Butkus in two weeks for vaccinations and a heartworm test. I watched as Butkus and Butch slowly walked back to the pickup with the log chain wrapped again around his neck. I wondered if they would come back in two weeks.

To my surprise, they did return in two weeks. Butkus had done extremely well and seemed happy to see me again. We did our exam, and we discussed heartworm prevention. However, when we did our heartworm test, it was positive. We proceeded to do our normal pre-testing for heartworm treatment, and fortunately, his blood work and x-rays were normal. Our heartworm treatment consists of injecting a toxic drug into the loin muscle over two days. The drug was quite expensive, and it could be very irritating to the tissue where it was injected. Butch did not hesitate for me to initiate the expensive treatment. When we injected this drug into most patients, they reacted by crying or attempting to bite in response to the injection. Butkus was different. When I injected the drug, he showed absolutely no response. Butkus confirmed that he was one tough junkyard dog.

My next visit from Butkus was early on a Friday morning. Butch had called and wanted to bring Butkus right over as he had broken his leg. As the auto repair shop was closing, Butkus had spotted a squirrel across the street and went on a chase to capture the squirrel. Just as he was running across the road, a car hit him and literally dragged him down the street for twenty feet. Butkus got right up and started walking back to the shop. However, Butch noticed that his right hock was scraped, and the bone was sheared away, exposing his hock joint. Butkus did not seem concerned, but Butch felt obligated to help good ole Butkus.

Butch did not want to bother me at night as the clinic was now closed. I knew Butch would not have hesitated to spend the extra money for an emergency visit, but Butkus seemed comfortable and decided not to call me. Instead, one of Butch's friends came by and said he could help. He saw the bones and the inner joints totally exposed. It was like looking at a picture of the hock in a veterinary anatomy book. They decided that if the bone was broken, they should apply a cast. So they went to a local hardware store and bought some plaster of Paris compound. They mixed it up according to directions and applied the plaster directly onto the bones inside of the joint. There was no application of any gauze or bandage to protect the bones inside of the joint.

So when I saw Butkus the next morning, he had hard plaster molded around his right hock. It was very hard and immovable. I told Butch we had our work cut out for us as we needed to chisel out all of the plaster and clean out the joints. Butch apologized profusely for their medical decision and insisted I do whatever I could to help Butkus. I anesthetized Butkus and spent ninety minutes chiseling out the plaster and flushing the hock joint profusely with sterile saline solution. I did not close the wound but left it open for drainage and applied an antibiotic dressing. I called Butch later that day and advised him that Butkus would need to return daily for a change to his dressing. Butch thanked me profusely and said he would be in to pick him up shortly.

As I again watched Butch and Butkus leave the clinic for the third time, I observed that Butkus again walked slowly without a limp and carried his heavy log chain around his neck to the pickup. He then jumped up into the pickup bed for his ride home.

Butkus was one tough, junkyard dog.

UNIQUE PATIENTS CALL FOR UNIQUE TREATMENTS

One thing unique to a veterinary clinic is that each day is different and one never knows what may walk through the door asking for your help. It also requires that one be resourceful and try to solve each patient's problem in best possible way. I found that one can't always go by the book because many times, the treatments required are not in anyone's book.

One morning, I saw a longtime client whose pet was quite ill. Her little pet, Jane, was quite lethargic, and she was oozing pus from her vaginal canal. These are typical symptoms of a pyometra infection where the uterus becomes infected and filled with pus. The bacterial toxins in the uterus become quite toxic, and the only way to save the patient is to do an immediate hysterectomy to remove the source of the infection. I recommended to Jane's owner that we do an immediate ovariohysterectomy to get rid of her infection and save her life. Jane's owner said that would be fine. However, Jane was currently being used in a high school play as a prop. She said it was very important that she recover so she would be ready for the stage that night.

I explained that we needed to do emergency surgery and that she was already toxic from the infection. There was always a possibility that she might not survive the surgery or she might not be strong enough to be carried on stage that evening. Jane's owner again begged me to do everything I could to help Jane survive and be ready for that night's stage performance.

So I took Jane to surgery with some concern that everything would work out. I masked Jane down with gas anesthesia, gave her fluids, and proceeded with the surgery. I found the uterus to be quite large and filled with a lot of pus. Surgery went well, and as soon as we closed the incision, the vet tech wrapped her in a warm towel and continued to monitor her recovery.

To my relief, Jane woke up very fast, and the combination of removing the infection and the fluids to flush out the bacterial toxins caused her to respond to normal very quickly. I called Jane's owner, who was ecstatic that things went well. I gave the okay for Jane to go on stage that night as long as they carry her and not cause a lot of undue stress.

By the way, Jane was not a dog or a cat but a three-pound rat who was one of their family pets. She was in a high school play production, and she recovered so well that they even brought her out for a curtain call after she performed that night. I guess she lived up to the old adage, "The show must go on."

Another unusual pet was a three-foot bull snake that was presented to me when I was working at the emergency clinic. I never had a fondness for snakes, and if someone would call with a snake problem, I would happily refer them to other veterinarians who were more comfortable and more knowledgeable with them. However, on this Saturday afternoon when I was working at the emergency clinic, I did not have that option to refer them.

The owners of the snake had just fed their snake a mouse, which was the normal diet. In the process of attacking and swallowing the mouse, the lower mandible or jawbone separated more than usual, and the snake swallowed one half of its mandible. It is normal for the lower mandibles or jaw bones to separate so the snake can swallow large objects. However, they should not swallow their own jawbone.

My vet tech, Jim, was more comfortable working with snakes than I was, so fortunately, he handled the snake very well. We calculated the dose of ketamine to anesthetize the snake and gave the injection into the muscle belly of the snake. The snake became very relaxed, and I was able to extract the half of the mandible from the esophagus and bring it back to its normal position. I then took adhesive tape and taped the mouth shut and instructed the owner to remove the tape in one week. Fortunately, the snake had just finished eating, so he did not require another meal for another week. I was sure I was more relieved to have my experience finished with treating the snake more so than the owner.

Perhaps the smallest patient that was presented to me was a dwarf hamster with a fractured leg. This little hamster named Midgie belonged to a third generation client of mine who was a nine-year-old girl named Brenda. Brenda's parents and her grandparents were longtime loyal clients of mine. They loved animals and were very kindhearted in helping their pets and people.

One night, Brenda woke up at three in the morning to go to the bathroom. As she was walking by her hamster cage, she noticed that Midgie had his little leg caught in the bars of the cage. She woke up her parents, and they all rushed little Midgie to the emergency clinic. When they saw the clinician, he informed them that the leg of Midgie was so severely fractured that he would need to amputate the leg. Brenda cried and cried and insisted that they save the little leg on Midgie. The clinician insisted that there was no other possible solution. However, Brenda was not convinced and asked her parents to see me first thing in the morning.

So, at eight the next morning, I was presented with a hamster no bigger than the end of my thumb with a broken femur. Brenda's eyes were red and swollen, and her mother had a very concerned look on her face. I carefully examined Midgie and found the left femur not only severely fractured but also the tissue and blood supply to the leg were also severed. In fact, the only thing holding the dangling leg onto Midgie was a small piece of skin. I knew the only solution was to finish the amputation by trimming the remaining piece of skin.

I took a long deep breath and slowly tried to explain how it would be medically impossible to save the leg. My explanation of the importance of blood supply, etc., was going on deaf ears. Finally, Brenda's mom looked at me and asked if I could at least try. I hesitated for a few seconds and then realized that maybe they needed some time before we actually do the amputation. The nerves to the leg were severed as well as the blood supply, so there would not be any pain to attempt to treat the leg for one week. I consented to try a bandage for one week, and then we would recheck Midgie. Brenda and her mom were elated, and they thanked me profusely for trying to help Midgie.

I brought little Midgie back to the treatment room and had my assistant, Carrie, help me apply the bandage. I was very concerned that we could cause more damage to Midgie in applying the bandage as Midgie liked to bite whoever was holding him. I instructed Carrie to be extremely careful and didn't hold him too tight where we might cause some damage. I was also concerned the leg might completely fall off in the process of taping the leg. So we proceeded to carefully apply tape to the leg. Actually, we were taping the broken leg so it would not fall off. Carrie was doing a great job of holding Midgie as he was trying to bite us the entire time we were applying the tape. I was relieved that we were successful to apply the tape without causing any harm.

I followed Carrie as she brought back Midgie to the exam room. As we were just entering the exam room, Midgie was able to bite down on Carrie's hand. Carrie was surprised and reacted by throwing her hand upward and hurling little Midgie across the exam room. I had been so tense earlier with the taping, so when I saw little Midgie flying across the room, my emotions let go. And I started laughing. When I regained my composure, I realized how unprofessional I had been and picked up Midgie off the floor. Fortunately, Midgie appeared just fine, and there were no further injuries. I thought maybe that I had upset my loyal and longtime client. However, she simply said that Midgie did that all the time and she was sorry that she bit Carrie.

One week later, Brenda and her mom returned for their appointment. The leg had actually turned somewhat black, and one could tell that the leg was deteriorating. I took a small scissors and neatly trimmed away the remaining piece of skin. Midgie did well on three legs but continued to bite his owner whenever he could. And I never did develop a great love for treating hamsters.

SURPRISE, SURPRISE, SURPRISE

Every veterinarian has encountered medical situations that haven't turned out quite as expected. Some are for the good, and some are not so good. Every veterinarian in practice has been shocked to find a patient under his care who suddenly passed away unexpectedly and also those patients whom seem to make a miraculous recovery. Believe me, phone calls to owners who have lost their beloved pets unexpectedly can be one of the most difficult parts of the job. So I learned as a young veterinarian that you have to take the bad along with the good. The following are some of my notable surprises.

Fifi was a happy miniature poodle who loved everyone and also loved to eat. She belonged to Doris, who was a single lady who did not have any children. Therefore, Fifi was her family and very important to her. Doris worked at The Viking restaurant as a waitress and, as a result, would often bring home table scraps for Fifi when she came home. During my previous exams of Fifi, I would often mention that Fifi was putting on some extra weight and maybe the first thing we should do would be to cut out table scraps. Doris would always nod her head in agreement. However, I knew that she would have a really tough time taking away the pleasure of giving Fifi something special when she got home.

Early one Sunday morning when I was on emergency call, I received a frantic phone call from Doris around 3:00 a.m. As usual, around 1:00 a.m., Doris had come home from work at the restaurant and gave Fifi a lamb chop bone. Fifi eagerly went after the special treat, but suddenly, the lamb chop bone got lodged in Fifi's esophagus. Fifi was gagging and coughing but could not relieve herself from the obstruction. Finally, after two hours of gagging, Doris called me, asking for help. She was very apologetic and felt horrible that she had caused Fifi such horrible distress.

I met her at the clinic at 3:30 a.m. and found Fifi still gagging and choking. Doris was frantic and continued to apologize. I examined Fifi and discovered that I could palpate the bone in the esophagus in the neck just in front of the chest cavity. I knew that esophageal surgery would be difficult, and unfortunately, at 3:30 a.m. on a Sunday morning, I didn't have anyone to call to help me. I kept thinking about my different options and how I could relieve Fifi of her distress while I was feeling the bone in the neck. One of my options would be to anesthetize Fifi and attempt to push the bone down into the stomach, but I knew if the bone got lodged deeper into the chest cavity, that would make the situation even worse. This was before endoscopes were available, which would have been a much easier option today.

During this time of trying to come up with a good option, I continued to feel the bone through the neck, trying to assess the size of the bone. Doris had now stopped apologizing and became quiet. I could sense her extreme worry as I was in deep thought on how I was going to handle the situation. About that time, Fifi made a strong and loud cough, and to my surprise, the bone became dislodged onto the exam table. Doris screamed of joy and looked at me like I had performed a miracle. She gave me a hug and showered me with praises that I was the greatest vet of all time. Little did she know that I was the most surprised and relieved.

Another surprise came from our own family cat, Mandy. Mandy was a two-year-old female gray tabby who was very sweet. She would often sit on my lap at night when I watched television. When it was time for her annual vaccinations and exam, I would bring her to work with me for the day. So I brought Mandy with me to work this one Saturday morning. I did a thorough exam and took some blood to screen for any potential organ problems and gave her annual vaccinations. Then I placed her back into the cat carrier to bring her home.

When I brought Mandy home, I opened the cat carrier and found Mandy lifeless. At first, I thought she was just sleeping and relieved to be home. I hurriedly picked her up and found her totally limp. I grabbed my stethoscope and found there was not a heartbeat. I compressed on her chest for a while, hoping to get her heart started again. To say the least, I was totally shocked and in disbelief. How could my own cat who was just examined and who sat on my lap at night suddenly die? My curiosity led me to bring Mandy back to the clinic to do a postmortem exam.

I initially opened Mandy's abdomen and found no abnormalities. The liver, kidneys, pancreas, and all the intestines appeared completely normal. Then I opened her chest cavity and found the lungs and the heart appeared normal on the outside. However, when I opened the heart, I found that the chambers of the heart were small and the heart muscle was extremely thickened. This is a characteristic sign of feline hypertrophic cardiomyopathy. The heart muscle thickens and obliterates the heart chambers, causing a severe decrease in the cardiac output. I'm sure the stress of the car ride added to the sudden death but realized it would have happened sometime at home very soon. This condition is often found in young athletes who suddenly collapse and die. Most notably is Jim Fixx, the marathon runner, and Hank Gathers, the basketball star. Unfortunately, there is no easy way to diagnose this disease unless you do cardiac ultrasound. I now had firsthand experience on how my clients must feel when I have had to call and inform them that their pet had unexpectedly died.

Another big surprise came early in my veterinary career. I was in my second year of my career and becoming quite confident in my veterinary skills when I became quite humbled. It seemed like a morning routine at the clinic. I had a dog to be spayed, a cat to be spayed, and a dental procedure to do on a miniature schnauzer. I initially performed the dog spay, and it went very well as I now had about 200 spay surgeries under my belt and they were becoming very routine.

My next surgical patient was Penny. Penny was quite ornery and feisty. She had been found as a four-month-old kitten in downtown Wheaton. Her contact with people at that time was virtually nonexistent. As a result, she was not well socialized and was always afraid of people. During my first and only previous encounter with Penny at four months of age, she was extremely difficult to exam. I barely was able to get close enough to her to even listen to her heart, and I could not examine her abdomen as she was trying to bite and scratch me along with my assistant.

I knew the most difficult part of Penny's spay surgery would be to anesthetize her without any injuries to myself or my veterinary technician. Today, if one has a difficult cat to anesthetize, drugs are available to be given in the muscle to sedate them. Another method available today is to place the cat in a small airtight chamber and use gas anesthesia to sedate them. However, in 1972, the only method available was to place the cat in a cat bag, pull out the front leg through a precut hole, and give an intravenous injection.

So after struggling with Penny for about ten minutes, we were able to give her an IV injection of Pentothal, and I was on my way to another routine spay. I was relieved knowing the hard part was over. I made my routine abdominal incision and began my search for the uterus. Penny was a young skinny cat, so I didn't anticipate any problem finding the uterus. However, I didn't find the uterus easily. I displaced the intestines to one side and followed the usual path of the uterus from the kidney to the bladder, but I still could not find the uterus. Finally, after about ten minutes of searching, a light went on in my head. Maybe Penny was not a female! So I had the technician look under the drape and check under the tail for anatomy. Sure enough, Penny was a male, and both his testicles were hiding under the tail.

Humbled and shocked, I closed the abdomen and went ahead and neutered him. I kept thinking that I was going to look really stupid to the owners when I called to tell them that I tried to spay their male cat. I remember when I was in veterinary school hearing the professors telling about how many veterinarians have been caught spaying male cats and how important it is to do a thorough exam. I thought to myself how ridiculous that would be and that would never happen to me. However, I had now joined the prestigious "Spay a Male Cat" Club.

As soon as I finished Penny's surgery, I called her—I mean his owners. I explained the difficulty in anesthetizing him and the difficulty in doing a pre-op exam and slowly explained how I couldn't find the uterus. Then I explained that I had the veterinary technician look under the drape and check for the sex. To my relief, a loud burst of laughter from the client came from the telephone. They thought the incident was absolutely hilarious. My red face and shaky voice soon changed to a little smile. From that day on, I always did a thorough pre-op exam prior to surgery and always looked under the tail to check the sex.

I learned early in my career that honesty and being up-front with clients was always the best policy. I could not guarantee the outcome of each of patients, but I could always guarantee that I would do my best to help them with their medical problems.

PEPI IS GONE

Frank and Edith were one of my favorite clients. They were retired, and they were the proud owners of Pepi. Pepi was a sweet miniature poodle who loved his owners and everyone he came in contact with. Pepi loved attention from anyone, and he certainly was fortunate to receive full attention for many hours every day from Frank and Edith.

Whenever I entered the exam room, Frank and Edith would always have huge smiles on their face. I would greet Pepi, and his little tail would wag. And Frank and Edith's smiles seemed to get even bigger. While I was stroking the fur on the neck of Pepi, I would ask about their two children. Their daughter was unmarried and worked at a zoo as an animal technician. They would often tell me stories of interesting incidents with the zoo animals. Their son worked for Haliburton oil in Houston. He was married, but they had no children even though he had been married for ten years.

Frank was retired as a buyer for Sears, and Edith previously worked as an assistant at Wheaton North High School. It was quite apparent they had a strong love for one another and they shared their love for little Pepi. I was always impressed on how happy they were together and how much they enjoyed spending time with one another and Pepi.

When I would finish my exam and treatment for Pepi, Frank and Edith would shower me with gratitude and praise. They certainly made me feel very fortunate to be a veterinarian. I would always feel that I must have the best job in the whole world to have the privilege to treat Pepi.

One day, Pepi came to the clinic with only Edith. As I walked into the exam room, there were no smiles, and all the happiness that

I so enjoyed seeing with Edith and Frank was gone. Edith somberly told me of Frank's passing four weeks ago. She went on to explain how Frank was found dead in his bed one morning and how they sent the ambulance, but they couldn't save him. As a lump developed in my throat and tears began to flow down my cheeks, I asked about their children and how they were doing. Edith explained how both her children had stayed with her for ten days, but now they had to return to their homes to get back to their jobs.

As the next few years went by, Edith would continue to come to the clinic with Pepi, but she didn't bring her smile that I was so accustomed to seeing. She missed Frank terribly and told me how Pepi was her only friend now. My previous appointments that always brought me smiles was now replaced with lumps in my throat and tears. When I would talk to Pepi and rub the fur around his neck that he always enjoyed, I would notice a partial smile from Edith. It was apparent that Pepi was her whole world.

One day as I was getting ready to leave the clinic for a quick lunch, I heard someone shout from the front of the clinic, "Help me! Help me!" Our receptionist, Lynn, recognized Edith and that she was carrying Pepi. Lynn quickly put her in an exam room, and I quickly met her with Pepi in her arms. Edith continued to say, "Please help Pepi. Help Pepi." I quickly unfolded the towels that Pepi was wrapped in and found Pepi stiff and cold. I knew, of course, that Pepi was gone. I didn't know how I was going to break the news to Edith, so I took out my stethoscope and listened to the chest. I held the stethoscope on the chest for a long time, trying to muster the courage to deliver the dreadful news.

Finally, I decided to tell her that Pepi was gone. Instead of more tears, Edith continued to plead, "Please help Pepi. Please help Pepi. I know you can help Pepi." I continued to tell her that Pepi was gone, and I brought in my stethoscope with an external speaker. I placed the stethoscope on the heart and said, "Edith, there is no heartbeat." Edith continued to plead, "Please help Pepi." I shined my penlight in Pepi's eyes and showed Edith there was no pupillary response. Edith continued to plead, "Please help Pepi." I then brought in my EKG machine and hooked up the leads to show there was no heart electrical activity. Edith continued to plead, "Please help Pepi."

As bad as I felt for Edith, I knew that somehow I was going to have to convince her that Pepi was gone. For some reason, I remembered when I would watch old cowboy movies on TV as a kid, they would place a mirror in front of the face to determine if someone had died. So I brought in a small mirror and placed it in front of Pepi's nose and told Edith calmly again that Pepi was gone. Edith then realized that she had lost Pepi and embraced me with a hug and a lot of tears. We then exchanged stories of Pepi and how special he was to everyone. After thirty minutes of talking about Pepi, Edith decided it was time to go home. I watched her walk slowly to her car empty-handed and only carrying Pepi's blankets. I knew that when she got home, it would be very difficult for her to walk into her home without anyone greeting her. Somehow, it didn't seem right to me that such a loving, wonderful lady should have to suffer such pain.

CATS DO HAVE NINE LIVES

Max was a feisty yellow tabby who belonged to a well-known and well-respected family in Wheaton. Max was adopted at the DuPage Animal Shelter when he was nine weeks old. The parents had adopted Max when their daughter, Jenny, came down with mononucleosis on her sixteenth birthday. Jenny's parents, Harry and Shirley, had grown up without the experience of having pets in their household, and they were always hesitant to adopt a pet. Finally, after years of Jenny begging to have a pet, they gave in knowing that they wanted to do something special for Jenny on her sixteenth birthday since she had mono.

My first introduction to Max was his initial exam the next day after being adopted. He was quite thin and had discharge from his eyes and a mucous discharge from his nostrils. His exam revealed he was suffering from respiratory virus, most likely chlamydia. His fecal exam showed a heavy infestation of roundworms, and tapeworm segments were found around his rectum. Fortunately, his feline leukemia blood test was normal. However, in spite of his ailments, Max was very spirited and feisty. When I first entered the exam room, Max started jumping up on my writing cabinet and knocked the alcohol bottle and thermometer holder over. Throughout his exam, Max continued to struggle to get off the exam table but did not resort to biting or scratching. I knew little Max was certainly going to change the lifestyle of his family.

We dispensed antibiotics for the respiratory infection, administered worm medications, and discussed what foods Max should be given. We discussed the proper way to prepare a litter box and possibly the need to have his front feet declawed. After answering all their questions, they were ready to take Max home and return in four weeks for another vaccination and an exam.

However, the next day, Shirley called me about Max. He wasn't eating and seemed to be a bit quiet. I was concerned about a vaccine reaction, so I had Max come right over to the clinic. On my exam, I found raw sores at the back of his lips. I knew Max suffered the injury from biting into an electrical cord. I advised them to kitten-proof the house as much as possible and possibly try coating the electrical cords with bitter apple.

The next day, Shirley again called me about Max. This time, he was found crawling up the sheer curtains in the living room and leaving big tears in the fabric. We talked about declawing, and Shirley and Harry reluctantly agreed. They were concerned about causing a lot of pain postoperatively. I assured them that the recovery would be minimal and Max would be running around their house in a matter of days.

We performed Max's front declaw on a Thursday, and he recovered very well and went home the next day. That evening while Harry and Shirley were having dinner guests, Max jumped up onto the dining table during the dinner and knocked the flaming candles over. Fortunately, the fire was put out quickly, and there was no damage. I explained to Harry and Shirley that they should try and put some carpet tape on the counters to discharge Max from jumping up on the counters. Also, I suggested having a squirt gun handy to squirt Max when he would jump up on the counters. It was becoming apparent that Max was a challenge, and I was hoping that they had the perseverance to continue taking care of Max. However, I could see that they all really loved little Max and were also entertained by his antics.

When Max was eight months old, Shirley called because Max had not been eating all day and seemed a bit lethargic. Shirley and Jenny brought Max over to be examined, and Harry left work early and joined us at the clinic. I could tell that they were all very concerned as Max was not running around the exam room and jumping up on the table like he usually did. Shirley mentioned that Max had vomited twice that afternoon. My exam revealed a mild fever, and he was tender and swollen on palpation of his abdomen. An abdominal x-ray revealed the small intestines were bunched together in an accordion pattern. This is a typical sign of a string foreign body. A string can get caught as it passes through the intestine, and as the intestine tries to push it through, the intestine becomes bunched together in an accordion pattern. I explained the need to do immediate surgery before the intestine perforates and causes severe peritonitis and death. Max's family had tears in their eyes, and they told me to do everything I could to save Max.

We started Max's surgery early that evening. After opening the abdomen, I found the accordion pattern of the intestines and discovered that it seemed to start in the stomach. I incised into the stomach and found sewing thread in a ball in the stomach. However, when I pulled on the ball of thread, Max would raise his head. We checked and rechecked the level of anesthesia, and it was good. So I had my surgical tech look under the tongue of Max. Lo and behold, the string was wrapped around the base of the tongue and partially embedded into the tongue, so it was difficult to see. My surgical tech cut the thread, and then I could easily remove the ball of thread from the stomach. The thread was also partially embedded into the intestines, so I had to make six other incisions in the small intestine. Fortunately, there were no perforations in the intestine.

After closing all the incisions and the abdomen, my surgical tech monitored Max while I went to the waiting room to explain to the family what we found. They were relieved that Max made it through the surgery but were still concerned about his recovery. I assured them that I would check on Max several times during the night and let them know if there were any complications.

I checked Max at 10:00 p.m. and 1:00 a.m. At 1:00 a.m., Max was moving about and seemed quite comfortable. I removed his IV at that time as I was concerned it would get tangled up. When I came into the clinic at 7:30 a.m., Max was meowing and walking around the cage, trying to find a way to get out. I called his family and told them how well Max was doing. They were ecstatic and made arrangements to pick up Max later that day.

Over the next six months, the phone calls from Max's family were less frequent. I knew that Max was finally growing up and he was not as crazy as he was when he was a kitten. However, one

Saturday morning just as we turned the answering machine at 8:00 a.m., Shirley called the clinic and was screaming, "He's alive. He's alive!" Our receptionist, Nancy, who answered the phone, could not determine what was going on, so she had me come to the phone. She continued to scream, "He's alive. He's alive!"

I, too, could not determine what was going on, so I said, "Bring Max right over." Shirley calmed down slightly and said, "We will be right there."

Within ten minutes, they arrived at the clinic, and Nancy brought them into the exam room immediately. I walked in expecting something horrible had happened to Max. Instead, Max was jumping up on the counters and moving around like he usually did. Eventually, Shirley and Harry calmed down to explain what had happened. The previous evening, Harry and Shirley were leaving their home to go out to dinner. As they were backing out of the driveway and lowering the garage door, Max ran into the garage as the door came down. They stopped the car and rushed to help Max, but he was totally limp and unresponsive. They cried and cried and felt so responsible for Max's demise. They called their daughter, Jenny, and gave her the horrible news, and she said she would come by early on Saturday morning to give her goodbye to Max. So they placed Max in a paper grocery bag and put him in the garage where it was cooler.

Jenny came by early the next morning to say her goodbye. As the family prepared to bring Max over to the clinic for cremation, Shirley opened the kitchen door to the garage and found Max running about the garage and exploring every nook and cranny of the garage. Shirley screamed like she saw a ghost, and Harry and Jenny came running into the garage. At that moment, Shirley called Village Animal Clinic and screamed, "He's alive! He's alive!"

The emotions of Max's family that weekend went from total sadness and despair to extreme joy and happiness. Yes, Max had succeeded in changing the lives of a family who didn't think they wanted a pet to one who cherished their four-legged friend with all their hearts. Another example of the power of the human-animal bond.

STEPPING UP TO BE A MIDWIFE

Katy was a loving three-year-old golden retriever who loved everybody. Her signature greeting was to look up at anyone who met her while fanning her tail repeatedly. When I entered the exam room and greeted Katy and pet her behind her ears, she would lie down submissively and encourage me to rub her under belly. She was one of my patients who would literally drag her owner through the front clinic door as she couldn't wait to greet everyone in the clinic.

Katy's family consisted of Jake, an eight-year-old boy; Sarah, a ten-year-old girl; and their mother, Julie, who had lost her husband to leukemia two years earlier. Years earlier, I always enjoyed visiting with her husband as he had been an avid runner like myself and had ran many marathons. It was always ironic to me that someone so fit would succumb to cancer.

Julie had decided to breed Katy to produce puppies, which she could sell to some of her friends who adored Katy. She was also hoping to make some extra money to build up the college fund for her two children.

After Katy had been bred, Julie and her children were counting the days until they could find out if Katy's pregnancy had taken. Unlike human medicine, there isn't a blood or a urine test that conclusively determines pregnancy. Also, ultrasound was not available at that time. So the only way to diagnose pregnancy is to palpate the abdomen, find the horns of the uterus, and palpate lumps within the uterus. It takes twenty-eight days from breeding for the fetus to grow to the size of a robin egg and therefore, large enough to be palpated.

When Julie and her family showed up with Katy on the twenty-eighth day, they were anxious to hear if their prized dog was going to have puppies. As I entered the room with Katy, I did my usual, rubbing her fur behind her ears while Katy's tail was furiously wagging. She then cooperatively laid down on the exam room floor like she knew what I needed to do next. I started to palpate her abdomen to find the uterus. Like many golden retrievers, Katy carried some extra abdominal fat, so it was difficult to find the uterus and the diagnostic robin eggs that would confirm the pregnancy. I was beginning to fear that I would not be able to make a determination of her pregnancy when I suddenly found two characteristic robin egg lumps within the uterus. I looked up at Katy's family, and I believed my facial expression had already given away the positive diagnosis when I said, "She's pregnant." Julie, Sarah, and Jake were ecstatic, and suddenly Katy was swarmed with hugs. I got my calendar out and determined her due date. We then talked briefly about the preparation for Katy's whelping and nutritional care for the next five weeks of her pregnancy. We then scheduled an appointment for a recheck and an x-ray on the fifty-eighth day of her pregnancy.

At her next appointment, I examined Katy and found that she was doing extremely well. She had gained about eighteen pounds, which seemed to be more than I was comfortable with, but otherwise, she was in good health. We took an abdominal x-ray at that point to determine the number of pups and their size. The x-ray revealed five large fetuses packed within the abdomen. I was somewhat concerned that Katy might have difficulty delivering her pups naturally. I gave her my guidelines for whelping, which was to wait four hours of labor for the first pup and two hours of labor for the following puppies. I explained that she should take Katy's temperature every twelve hours until whelping began. If her temperature would drop two degrees, that would signal that labor would begin in twelve to twenty-four hours. I advised them to call if they notice any development and keep us informed of her progress.

Five days later, Julie called and said that Katy's temp had dropped two degrees. No labor contractions were noted as yet. Our advice was to continue to keep us informed. That night around midnight, my answering service called to let me know that Katy was having trouble whelping. This was happening in the late 1970s, so emergency clinics had not been established yet. I did have to explain to the people working at the answering service what the term *whelping* actually meant. Earlier, I had an experience where someone called the answering service and said their dog was whelping. The lady on the service thought she said yelping and curtly said, "I don't think that is a reason to disturb the doctor in the middle of the night."

When I called Julie back, she informed me that she found Katy with one dead puppy and she was having contractions with no success. I told her I would meet her at the clinic in fifteen minutes. When she arrived, Katy was not wagging her tail, and I could see she was in distress. I did a vaginal exam and was unable to palpate a pup. My suspicion was that the pup was too large to enter the birth canal. I decided to give Katy an IV injection of oxytocin to strengthen her contractions. If the injection did not work in thirty minutes, we would need to do an emergency Cesarean.

After thirty minutes, Katy was still in distress and unable to deliver her pups. I told Julie we needed to do an emergency Cesarean to have a chance to save her remaining pups. I asked Julie if she could assist by taking the puppies as I delivered them and rub and clean them up as I handed them to her. She said she would do anything she could to help. I rolled Katy onto the surgery table, shaved her belly, and did a surgical scrub. I then gave her a light amount of anesthesia along with a local injection into the belly to numb the surgical site. It is important to keep the levels of general anesthesia as low as possible to increase the chance of survival for the puppies.

I gave Julie a quick lesson on how to catch the pups, rub them, and stimulate their breathing to increase their chance for survival. I proceeded with my incision into the abdomen and lifted the heavy uterus out of her belly to get ready to make an incision into the uterus. Since the pups were located in each horn of the uterus, it is normal to make the uterine incision along the top of the body of the uterus so you can remove all the pups with one incision. I made my incision and milked out the first pup. I removed the placental membranes over the mouth and nose of the pup and dropped the puppy into the towel, which Julie was holding. Julie seemed a little white in the face but otherwise was anxious to do what she had to do. There was several moments of silence, so I told Julie to rub the puppy's chest briskly and hold the pup firmly and swing the puppy downward to help clear the airway. At that point, the puppy started crying, which was music to our ears. I now had an experienced OB nurse who now was helping me with the successful delivery of the next three live pups.

I had Julie put the squealing puppies in a basket with warm towels, and I continued with my surgery. It took me about twenty minutes to carefully suture the uterine incision, the abdominal wall, and the skin layer. Julie and the pups were in the adjoining room, and all I could hear were the puppies. After finishing my surgery, I removed the endotracheal tube and cleaned up Katy's belly. I lifted her down to some blankets on the floor to allow her to continue to wake up from the anesthesia. I was anxious to see the pups, so I went into the adjoining room and found all the puppies to be doing extremely well.

However, Julie was sitting on the floor propped up against the wall. She had no color to her face, and her eyes were fuzzy. I asked her what was happening, and she informed me that she always fainted at the sight of any blood. I said, "How in the world did you help deliver these puppies?" Julie said that she knew she had no choice but to step up and perform her duty. However, when everything was all over, her mind could not control her emotions anymore, and she collapsed, but not until she knew that Katy and her puppies were all okay.

I learned that night how strong the human will can be in times of need.

YOU CAN'T JUDGE A BOOK BY ITS COVER

By and large, the veterinary clients that I have met over my forty-two years of practice are very kind and warm-hearted people who would do everything they can to help their beloved pets. However, I have seen many clients that go about their objective to help their pets in a different way. One thing that I learned early in my veterinary career is that you could not predict what clients would do to help their pets. Even if the client was a longtime established client, I was still unable to predict what their decisions would be for their pets. Therefore, I would always present the best possible treatment for their pets no matter what their financial status appeared to be. If they were not agreeable to the best option, then I would discuss other possibilities.

I learned early on in my veterinary career that the ability to pay for veterinary services did not always correlate into what level of care they would pay for their pets. One week, I was presented with a two-year-old male cat who had developed a urethral blockage for the second time. A change in the diet had not prevented an obstruction from the first blockage. Therefore, we suggested that we do a surgery called a perineal urethrostomy to prevent another blockage. This procedure, in effect, shortens and enlarges the urethra to prevent another obstruction. At this time, this procedure cost approximately $300. I thought that the owners of this cat would schedule this procedure as soon as possible as the father of the family was a physician and the wife was a nurse, and I thought they certainly had the funds to pay for the surgery. To my surprise, they elected to put the cat to sleep as they didn't want to spend any more money on their cat.

Later that week, I was presented with an Irish setter who had been hit by a car. His vitals were normal, and there were no internal injuries. However, the Irish setter had sustained a severely comminuted fracture of his femur where the mid-shaft of his femur was broken up into four pieces. I had repaired a lot of fractured femurs with an intramedullary pin and cerclage wires, but this type of fracture would require special equipment performed by an orthopedic specialist. The owner of the dog was a retired railroad worker who lived alone. I expected him to say that he would have to euthanize his dog. Instead, he went to the bank and got a loan for $1,200 to use for the orthopedic surgery. I learned a valuable lesson: The value of the pet and the owner's willingness to pay is stronger than the owner's ability to pay.

I also learned one other dark side about running the business of a veterinary clinic. Early in my veterinary career, I was presented with a twelve-week-old German shepherd puppy named Duke who was severely dehydrated, vomiting, and weak. The previous two days, the owner reported that Duke had diarrhea but was still eating and drinking. I did not know much about the owner. His name was Rex, but he refused to divulge his occupation on the client information sheet. His address was listed as a post office box number, so I did not know even where he lived. However, Rex seemed to be well off as he always wore nice clothes, and I saw him pull into the clinic parking lot driving a late model Cadillac.

Rex first brought Duke into the clinic on a Friday afternoon. Duke was not eating and very weak. I performed some initial x-rays and drew blood for the lab. The x-ray showed a large swollen intestine, which appeared as a foreign body lodged in the intestine or an intussusception. An intussusception was a condition where one loop of intestine telescopes into the adjoining intestine, similar to pulling a sock through to the end. Upon palpation of the abdomen, I could palpate a large firm mass within the intestine. I realized at this point that Duke would need surgery either for the abdominal foreign body or the intussusception. I suggested that we skip the barium series to confirm the diagnosis and take Duke straight to surgery. I was concerned if we waited much longer for the surgery, we would not have a chance to save Duke.

I discussed the problem with Rex, who readily agreed to have the surgery done immediately. I stressed the fact that Duke was quite ill and he could die in spite of our best efforts to save him. Rex insisted that I do everything I could to save Duke. He said money was no object.

I started Duke's surgery that Friday night. Upon opening up his abdomen, I found Duke to be worse off than I expected. Not only did he have a six-inch intussusception but also the intestine was turning black and developing necrosis at the site of the intussusception. The intussusception had caused the blood supply to that portion of the intestine to become compromised, and as a result, the tissue was dying. Therefore, I had to remove approximately fifteen inches of intestine. This procedure called an anastomosis requires that you remove all the diseased intestine and hook up the new openings of the intestine carefully so you preserve the blood supply as well as making sure that you have no leaks in hooking up the new intestines. After two hours of surgery and testing the suture line of the anastomosis, everything looked good, so we were able to close the abdomen.

Because Duke was so weak, I knew that even though he survived the surgery, we were not out of the woods to survive what he had been through. When I left the clinic at 10:00 p.m., Duke was still mostly unconscious. I kept the IV fluids going, wrapped him a warm blanket, and went home for a few hours of sleep. At 1:00 a.m., Duke was barely conscious and had not moved at all for the past three hours. I knew the recovery was not going to be quick and easy.

When I arrived at the clinic later that morning, Duke still had not changed much. I called Rex again and explained the gravity of the situation, and he again said, "Do everything you can to save Duke." I explained it might be 3–4 days before we would be able to send Duke home if he survived.

Each day, Duke showed some gradual improvement. By Wednesday, now five days out from his surgery, we were able to get Duke to eat a small amount of A/D food, which is very tasty and high in calories. The next day, Duke ate even more A/D food and passed a small amount of stool. So I called Rex and said we could send Duke home as long as he can give him some oral antibiotics.

Rex came by later that day driving into the clinic in his late model Cadillac. Rex again was well dressed, and because he was a nice-looking man, he could easily have been on the cover of GQ magazine. After going over all the discharge instructions, Rex proceeded to the checkout counter to pay his bill. I had given Rex a rough estimate of the charges before we did the surgery but had not added the extra charges for the lengthy hospitalization. Rex briefly looked at the bill and said he would be right back. The receptionist believed he was going out to his Cadillac to get his checkbook. So she said that would be fine. However, Rex placed Duke in his car and quickly drove out of the clinic parking lot. We then thought that he had to run to the bank and get some cash. However, he did not return that day or the next few days.

Our calls to Rex's house were not answered. I even called and left a message saying we needed to recheck Duke and remove his sutures. Again, there was no response, and we all slowly realized that we had been taken by this smooth-talking, well-dressed man driving a late model Cadillac.

For many years following this incident, when I have a client who says "Do everything you can" and "Money is no object," I wonder if they are saying that because they have no intention of paying their bill. We did not receive training in veterinary school on how to manage the business of a veterinary clinic, but the school of hard knocks was giving me a rapid crash course.

SECOND CHANCE FOR MAGGIE

Maggie was a three-year-old standard poodle with a lot of energy and a lot of love. She liked to run because not only did she have a lot of energy but she also loved people and would often run to visit the neighbors down the street. Her behavior was rewarded as the escape from her home would give her more attention and treats from the neighbors.

Maggie's family was a very busy professional couple with three small children. The husband, Phil, was a pilot for American Airlines. The wife, Sandy, was an ER nurse at Central DuPage Hospital. They had three beautiful girls, ages one, three, and six years. To say the least, Phil and Sandy kept very busy with their irregular work schedules and looking after their three daughters.

My first introduction to Maggie was an emergency. Maggie had been out of the yard running and meeting people when she crossed Highway 59 and was hit by a car. Phil rushed Maggie over to the clinic while toting his three daughters as well. Upon examination, Maggie seemed fairly stable, but her breathing was mildly labored. Her vitals and color seemed normal. Abdominal x-rays were normal, and there were no signs of any fractures. However, her chest x-rays showed pneumothorax. Pneumothorax is a condition where the lung will partially collapse. It is often caused by trauma to the chest area where the lung spaces will rupture, and likewise, the lung will partially collapse. Because the pneumothorax was mild, surgery was not required, and chest drains were not needed to correct the condition. I knew that in a few days with proper rest, Maggie's lung would heal and the pneumothorax would go away. I sent Maggie on home later that day with medications for pain, antibiotics to prevent infection in the wounds on her skin, and enforced rest.

I called the next day to check on Maggie's progress. She was moving slowly but eating and doing well. I advised them to continue the medications and keep me informed on how she continued to do. They were advised to return in three days for a follow up x-ray to make sure the pneumothorax was resolving.

However, the next day, Sandy called me and was frantic. She was giving Maggie the Hycodan syrup for pain to Maggie with a spoon when Maggie quickly ingested the spoon and the syrup all at once. Sandy had tried to quickly remove the spoon from the mouth, but it was too late as she already had swallowed it.

I quickly took an abdominal x-ray to confirm what had happened. Sure enough, the entire spoon was visible within the walls of the stomach. It turned out to be an amazing x-ray as the spoon filled up the entire stomach. I often used this x-ray when I would give talks to grade school children at their schools. The kids always enjoyed seeing the big spoon inside the dog's stomach.

The chest x-ray showed the pneumothorax had improved but was not totally resolved. So I decided to postpone Maggie's stomach surgery for two more days to let her condition improve. I felt that because the spoon was so large, it would not pass out of the stomach into the intestine, so there should be no harm in waiting for two days to do the surgery. Maggie did return in two days for the surgery, and everything went well.

About one year later from the car accident, Sandy had dropped off a urine sample on her way to work at Central DuPage Hospital. Our veterinary technician had performed the urinalysis and found no abnormalities. Sandy had told the vet tech that Maggie was wetting in the house about once a week. Sandy thought she was having behavioral problems because they were now sending their daughters to a day care facility and no one was home during the day. I recommended that we exam Maggie and see if we could find a physical cause for the abnormal urination. Sandy said she would watch Maggie and see what happens.

Two weeks later, Sandy brought another urine sample to the clinic. This time, the urinalysis showed a very mild increase in red blood cells on the sediment, but no bacteria was seen. I called Sandy with the report and suggested we should exam Maggie for a possible bladder infection, vaginitis, hormonal incontinence, or possibly a bladder stone. Sandy mentioned her schedule was full and asked if we could just start her on antibiotics to clear up a possible bladder infection. I agreed and dispensed Clavamox for two weeks and advised to return with a urine sample in two weeks.

Four weeks later, Sandy brought another urine sample in for analysis. Maggie had done well for two weeks, but now she urinated in the house again. The results of the urine sample was the same, a mild increase in the red blood cells. Sandy asked if we could try another antibiotic, so we sent home Baytril for two weeks. I again reluctantly agreed as Sandy said she did not have time to bring Maggie in for an exam.

Six weeks later, Sandy called and reported that Maggie had actually gotten worse. She was having urinary accidents almost daily and causing damage to their carpets. Sandy was sure it was a behavioral problem because she only had accidents during the day when the house was empty. Sandy was very upset and asked about euthanasia. She said she could not keep a dog urinating in the house with three little girls. I explained briefly the process of euthanasia and options for cremation. Again, I said, "Let's take a look at Maggie. Maybe there is a physical cause, and we should make sure." Finally, Sandy agreed to bring Maggie in for an exam.

The following Saturday morning, Sandy and Phil brought in Maggie for an appointment. They had gotten a babysitter for their three daughters as they were prepared to say goodbye to Maggie. Both Phil and Sandy had tears in their eyes as I walked into the exam room.

Maggie was her normal happy, loving self and wagged her little tail as I entered the room. I was thinking how difficult this would be to euthanize Maggie as she wagged her tail and wanted to lick you in the face. The vet tech had already done the urinalysis, which basically had not changed. I decided to do an extensive exam, hoping to find some physical cause for her wetting. However, when I started to palpate the abdomen, I found a large mass in the area of the urinary bladder. I immediately did an abdominal x-ray, which confirmed a large tennis ball-size stone in the urinary bladder. It was probably one of the largest bladder stones that I had ever seen. In fact, I often used this x-ray of the large bladder stone along with the spoon in the stomach for my school presentations.

When I showed the x-ray to Phil and Sandy, they were ecstatic that we could resolve the urinary problem with the surgical removal of the stone. Maggie recovered well following the surgery and never had another urinary accident in the house. I knew both Phil and Sandy felt guilty about their refusal to bring Maggie into the clinic earlier for an appointment. I never brought the subject up again as I knew they already felt very bad. However, when Sandy brought in Maggie for her suture removal ten days later, she said as they were walking out the door, "Next time we will listen to you."

ALWAYS PICK UP YOUR UNDERWEAR

Dogs are a lot like children. They are curious creatures, and many have an oral fixation to chew up objects and swallow them. Cats are curious creatures as well, but they don't have the oral fixation to chew and swallow everything in sight. One exception of that was Tigger. Tigger was a yellow tabby who liked to play with anything. Tigger was presented to me for vomiting, not eating, and becoming lethargic. My exam revealed mild dehydration and a ropey feel to the intestines. I took some x-rays of Tigger's abdomen and discovered an accordion pattern to the intestines. This finding usually means that there is a linear foreign body in the intestine. Usually, we find string or thread stuck in the stomach, and the normal movements of the intestine causes the intestine to bunch up in an accordion pattern. Surgery is indicated immediately as eventually the thread or string will cut through the wall of the intestine and cause peritonitis, leading to the death of the patient.

 Therefore, we took Tigger to surgery to remove the string or thread, which was embedded in the intestine. Upon opening the abdomen, I found thread from the stomach throughout most of the small intestine. I made an incision into the small intestine about halfway through the length of the intestine, and I was successful in removing the thread from the lower half of the intestine. Fortunately, the thread had not perforated the wall of the intestine. I then pulled the thread that went up to the stomach and noted that Tigger's head was moving up and down.

 I initially thought maybe Tigger was waking up from the anesthesia, but all of our anesthesia monitors showed that Tigger was well anesthetized. I was starting to freak out when I realized that every time I pulled on the thread, Tigger's head would raise up. So I had my veterinary technician look under the tongue of Tigger, and sure enough, she found the thread embedded around the base of the tongue. I had my tech cut the thread, and I was able to pull the thread out successfully through the intestinal incision. From that day on, I always check thoroughly under the tongue with any patient showing intestinal distress.

Pica is defined as the persistent and compulsive eating of substances that are basically nonnutritive. Dogs develop this trait mainly because of boredom and anxiety. Young dogs are like young children in that they have a lot of energy and require a lot of exercise. Many families today are too busy to provide adequate exercise for their dogs. As a result, they develop an oral fixation to swallow and eat objects out of boredom.

Socks, a young Old English Sheepdog puppy, was a classic example of the benefit of exercise. Socks belonged to a young couple who were both working full time. One day, they had delivered pea gravel in their backyard to provide a place for Socks to urinate without burning the grass. The next morning, Socks was let out in their backyard while the young couple were getting ready for work. Socks had so much pent up energy that she began to swallow a large amount of pea gravel. The young couple brought Socks inside to put in her cage and went off to work. They did not realize what trouble their beloved Socks had done. When they arrived home around 5:00 p.m., Socks was quite sick. She was showing nonproductive vomiting and acting lethargic. The young couple rushed Socks over to the clinic. My exam revealed a swollen tender abdomen, and the x-rays confirmed that she swallowed roughly three cups of pea gravel. Most of the pea gravel was trapped in the stomach, but a small amount was making its way to the small and large intestine. I knew she would not be able to pass such a large amount, so we took her to surgery to "clean her out."

Socks recovered well, and she went home the next day. I discussed with her parents what they could do to prevent such a disaster in the future. They agreed to take Socks on a fifteen-minute walk in the morning before they leave for work and another thirty-minute walk when they arrive home. They also signed Socks up for *Doggie*

Day Care to allow Socks to interact and play with other dogs while they were gone. Fortunately, the exercise plan worked, and Socks never showed signs of pica throughout her life.

However, that was not the case for Sparky, who was a young active Dalmatian that also loved to play and burn off some of his energy. Sparky belonged to a couple who owned a Brown's Fried Chicken restaurant. They both worked long hours at the restaurant. I initially met Sparky when he was also presented for nonproductive vomiting and lethargy. However, his exam did not reveal a swollen abdomen, and there was nothing visible on x-ray that indicated a blockage to the intestine. I therefore kept Sparky in the hospital and did a barium series to check for a blockage. Normally, barium travels through the stomach and into the colon in less than four hours. Our follow-up x-rays showed absolutely no movement, which confirmed an intestinal blockage. We therefore took Sparky to surgery immediately. Surgery revealed that a corncob was trapped in the duodenum, which is the first part of the small intestine from the stomach. Because the corncob was stuck where the stomach empties into the small intestine, there was no swelling of the small intestine. The surgery was successful, and Sparky went home the next morning. After explaining to the family what we found in Sparky, they confessed that they often brought *scraps* home from their restaurant for Sparky.

Even though I gave my "exercise speech" and the importance of not giving their dog table scraps, I saw Sparky again for the same problem. Within the next eight months, Sparky again was presented with the same exact problem, and both times, we removed a corncob from the duodenum. Apparently, the third time was a charm because after that period, either Sparky's owner wised up or maybe Sparky himself realized that eating corncobs was not safe.

Another way to prevent your pet from going through lifesaving intestinal surgery is the obvious. "Dog- and cat-proof your home." Just like with small children, one needs to be aware that your dog or cat may get into trouble and you need to lower the odds that your beloved pet will get himself into trouble.

Maxine was a young collie whose owners suffered through a life-changing event because they were not tidy. Her owners were a young couple, and they did not have any children as of yet. The father, Greg, worked at a car dealership in St. Charles. The mother, Lily, worked in a day care facility. They both were very nurturing to Maxine, so I was sure they would be great parents. When they first adopted Maxine from a shelter, they both would typically bring Maxine in on a Saturday morning. They both adored Maxine, and they were committed to provide the best possible care for their new addition.

Early one week day morning, Greg brought in Maxine because she showed nonproductive vomiting and she had stopped eating. Her abdomen was not tender or swollen, but the x-rays showed a possible foreign body within the stomach. Barium was again given, and they showed a definite foreign object within the stomach. Since barium seemed to stick within the foreign object, I suspected that it was some type of cloth. Upon exploratory surgery, I found all of her intestines were fine. But when I opened the stomach, I found a pair of red-laced panties. I removed the panties and did a routine closure of the stomach and the abdomen. Maxine stayed in the hospital one night, and she was scheduled to go home the next afternoon.

The next afternoon, Lily arrived and was glad that Maxine had done well and was ready to go home. I met with Lily and went over the discharge instructions. We had saved the panties, which I extracted from Maxine's stomach as I often do to show the owners what their dog had swallowed. However, as I removed the panties from the bag to show Lily, she turned pale and didn't say a word. Finally, after what seemed like several minutes, she said, "Those are not my panties."

I then realized what had happened and finally said, "Oh." In ten days, Lily brought Maxine back for suture removal. Maxine had recovered well from the surgery, but Lily was very quiet and continued to bring Maxine by herself.

I bet Greg had listened to his mother when she said, "Always pick up your underwear."

GO, CUBBIE, GO!

Cubbie was a young, rambunctious Old English Sheepdog puppy. He was brought in for his first exam and vaccination ten days earlier. His exam was normal. However, I noticed that he had a strong oral fixation, which caused him to constantly want to be chewing on something. The couple that had adopted him had brought several chew toys, which kept him somewhat occupied. However, during his exam, he was gently chewing on my fingers throughout the exam. Puppies are like young children in that they want to put everything in their mouth. I am sure Sigmund Freud would have a detailed scientific explanation, but in my opinion, the habit stems back to the calming effect of a puppy or a child nursing.

Cubbie's owners had previously euthanized their previous Old English Sheepdog of thirteen years. Being loyal Cub fans, their previous dog was named Ernie, after Ernie Banks, who was a Chicago Cubs hall of famer. I had treated Ernie the entire thirteen years of his life. Ernie was a very active dog like most Old English Sheepdogs but was always well behaved. Ernie's owners had controlled a lot of Ernie's energy by taking him for thirty-minute walks twice daily.

Cubbie's owners realized that their new puppy would need more exercise to somewhat control his hyperactivity. They signed Cubbie up for doggie day care to allow Cubbie to play with other dogs and be exercised while the owners both went off to work. Everything was going well with Cubbie until one Saturday, when they brought in some pea gravel to their backyard to set up a spot for Cubbie to go to the bathroom. After the delivery, Cubbie remained outside while the couple went inside to pay the delivery man and had a second cup of coffee. Within ten minutes, they looked outside and saw Cubbie swallowing the pea gravel like he hadn't eaten for over a week. They rushed outside to quickly stop Cubbie, not knowing how much gravel Cubbie had ingested.

Within the next thirty minutes, Cubbie began nonproductive vomiting. It continued and seemed to be getting worse. So they called Village Animal Clinic for help. Cubbie was presented immediately for exam. He was becoming more lethargic, and he didn't have the urge to chew on my hands and chew toys like his previous exam. An x-ray was taken immediately to access the amount of gravel that he had ingested. When the x-ray came out, I couldn't believe my eyes. There was approximately 2–3 cups of gravel in the stomach in addition to another 2 cups in the small and large intestine.

Knowing that the pea gravel in the stomach was so voluminous and impossible for Cubbie to vomit up, we decided that we should take Cubbie to surgery. Initially, I performed a gastrotomy where I opened up the stomach and literally dug out the pea gravel. I then closed the stomach and proceeded to milk out the gravel from the small intestine into the colon. I knew if the gravel made it to the large intestine, Cubbie should be able to pass the remaining rocks. So after spending several hours pushing each individual rock out from the small intestine to the large intestine, I closed the abdomen and allowed Cubbie to wake up.

During the recovery of Cubbie, we were all relieved that things went very well and that Cubbie was out of danger and he would recover very well. As Cubbie began to regain consciousness, we pulled the endotracheal tube that had been delivering the anesthetic gas. As with a lot of our surgical patients, the removal of the tube can elicit a cough. Cubbie then started coughing, and as luck would have it, the coughing caused Cubbie to push out some pea gravel with each cough. As fans often sang "Go Cubs Go" in celebration of a win, our staff started singing our own version of the famous celebratory song.

> Go, Cubbie, go! Go, Cubbie, go!
> Hey, Chicago, what do you say?
> Cubbie is going to poop today!

After watching the Cubs win the World Series and hearing the fans sing "Go Cubs Go," to this day, I always think of Cubbie when I hear the famous song when the Cubs won.

OMG! WHAT DID YOU EAT!

One of my golf buddies happened to be the obstetrician who delivered my youngest daughter, Dr. Amanda Healey. One day when we were golfing, I asked Jim how many babies he delivered. His response was that he delivered 7,000 babies over his career. I was amazed by the number, but it got me thinking about how many spay operations I had done over the years. Having your pet spayed is necessary to prevent your pet from going into estrus (heat) and to avoid the problems associated with heat periods, such as (1) the bloody mess of estrus, (2) avoiding an unplanned pregnancy, (3) preventing pyometra or an infected uterus, (4) avoiding the stressful effects of a false pregnancy, and (5) preventing mammary gland tumors.

I did some calculations and determined I had probably performed 10,000 spay operations over my forty-two year career. Therefore, most small animal veterinarians would be very comfortable doing a spay surgery since it is the most common.

However, sometimes things don't go quite as planned. One morning, I had a light load for surgery. A cat neuter, a skin tumor removal on a miniature schnauzer, and a spay on a four-year-old overweight beagle.

I started my surgery with the four-year-old beagle named Java. I had been recommending a spay for Java since she was six months of age. We anesthetized Java, and I proceeded to open the abdomen to find the ovaries and uterus. Since Java weighed fifteen pounds more than she should, my search for the uterus became a "Where's Waldo?" exercise. There was two inches of belly fat that had formed between the skin and the abdominal wall. Once I was able to find the linea alba, which is the juncture of each side of the muscles of the lower abdomen, I encountered a large amount of fat in the abdomen.

Most of the fat was located in the omentum, which is a fatty layer of tissue that helps regulate immune functions as well as storing fat.

So my easy routine spay operation had now became a search-and-destroy mission. I was so encumbered by the amount of fat that I had to lengthen my incision to help me find the ovaries and uterus. One trick I had learned was to look under the urinary bladder and find the body of the uterus and then follow each horn of the uterus up to the ovaries. I employed that method to grasp the ovaries and proceed to remove them. I had always prided myself on not irritating the soft tissue when I did surgery. Therefore, the patient would heal faster and with less pain. However, in my search-and-destroy mission, I probably irritated the tissue of the abdominal wall.

So I decided to close the abdomen with this new synthetic absorbable suture that was supposed to be stronger and not dissolve as quickly as regular catgut. By the way, catgut is not from cats but actually is made from the cap of sheep intestine. It is processed and designed to hold together for at least two weeks.

Things went well with the new suture material, and Java woke up and went home later in the day. Post-op instructions were sent home that included keeping Java quiet and start feeding a small meal that evening.

The next afternoon, Java's owner called and said that something was "sticking out" of the incision. I thought maybe a seroma had formed, which is a fluid pocket usually caused by irritation to the soft tissue. We had Java come over to the clinic right away to check out the swelling.

Upon Java's arrival and exam, I was shocked to see that the swelling was not a seroma but two open, chewed-off ends of the small intestine. To my disbelief, the incision had broken open, and we found two stumps of small intestine protruding through the incision. Java had actually chewed off the pieces of small intestine, which caused the intestinal contents to come out through the incision. My mouth had probably fallen to the floor, but I said we needed to take Java to surgery right away.

My surgery revealed that the suture material had not held its knots. Usually, a surgeon's knot is used, which is the standard knot.

However, this new material seemed stiffer than catgut, and the knots became untied. I knew that I was going to be challenged not only in finding the severed ends of the small intestine but also being able to do an intestinal anastomosis or suturing the ends of the intestine together.

I was able to find the two ends that had been chewed off, and my next step was to suture them together as well as preserve the blood supply to the intestines. I knew that Java would lose some of the intestine but didn't feel that it would be a significant loss. I knew the length of the small intestine was approximately seven times the length of the dog.

I closed the abdomen with stainless-steel wire sutures. They are the strongest, and they hold their knots very well. Unlike abdominal surgery on humans, we don't have the luxury of the patient being quiet and not putting stress on the incision.

When Java was waking up from the anesthesia, she vomited up eighteen inches of small intestine. I was amazed that Java would not only chew her own small intestine but swallow eighteen inches of intact small intestine.

I had Java's owner come in the next day for a checkup. She already had eaten a good meal that morning, and she seemed to feel fine. I told the owner that Java might have to eat more often and might lose some weight because of the shortened small intestine. However, six months later on a routine exam, Java had actually gained another five pounds and was doing great.

Java lived a long life of thirteen years. My "take home message" was that as long as you have the ability to eat, you will do fine and overcome any adversity.

THE SAN FRANCISCO TREAT

As a parent who has been partly responsible for raising three children, I have always thought that it is important to teach your children to develop a good work ethic by being responsible for chores around the house. I have always felt the responsibility of a parent to demonstrate and teach your children good habits to help them be successful in life.

I learned this from my parents growing up on a pig farm in Iowa. My dad expected me to help on the farm like most farm kids. I remember my first chore was to mow the grass around the house when I was eight years old. Unfortunately, we didn't have a power mower at the time. Instead, we had a push reel-type mower. I was never a big kid, so the handle of the mower was as high as I was. And because it was difficult to push the mower, I had to lean into the lower part of the handle to be able to get the mower to work.

As I got older, my jobs and responsibilities became more difficult. As a teenager, my parents never gave me a curfew to be home at a certain time. However, it was expected that you would be up the next morning at 6:00 a.m. to do your chores. The lessons learned were invaluable to me as I became a veterinarian.

So I tried to instill the same work habits in my three children. My oldest child, Wade, started mowing the grass at the clinic when he was ten years old. One summer day, he finished the mowing, so he came inside of the clinic to cool down. It was an extremely busy day, and we were behind on our appointments. I was busy tail docking a litter of Doberman pups. The veterinary technician was holding each pup so I could cut each tail. About that time, an emergency walked through the front door, so the vet tech was called away to help the other veterinarian. Wade then walked into the treatment room, so

I asked him if he would hold the puppy for me. In my haste to get the puppies tail docked, I didn't explain to Wade what I was doing. Instead, I grabbed my operating scissors and cut off the puppy's tail. Wade, seeing what I had done, yelled, "Dad, you cut off the tail," and became very upset with me. Two of the receptionists came running back to the treatment room to see what all the yelling was about. As one could imagine, I had some serious explaining to do. I learned my lesson that "haste makes waste" and that I needed to explain my intentions well.

My youngest daughter, Amanda, started working at the clinic when she was in junior high. She would come in to clean the kennels and clean the floors. As she got older, she then started to work as a receptionist and eventually, a technician. I have always felt one of the reasons for her success is that she started working on the ground floor and knows exactly the importance of each position of the clinic.

One summer, my oldest daughter, Jody, was looking for a job for a few months before she started law school. Jody didn't pursue a career into anything medical for a reason. She did not like anything bloody and would cringe if I described anything medical to her. We needed a receptionist at work at the time, so she thought she could handle doing the receptionist work as long as she wasn't required to help out "in the back."

One Saturday when we were getting ready to close, a collie was presented that was very sick. He was weak, depressed, and not eating. Jody was working the front desk, and Amanda (Dr. Healey) was working in the back as a veterinary technician. I examined Laddie and found a few maggots around the rectum. So Amanda and I took our electric clippers and started to shave the fur more extensively around the rectum to evaluate the extent of the maggot infestation. Much to our surprise, Laddie was infested heavily with the maggots, and they were beginning to eat the flesh from the top of the pelvic area to the groin underneath. Laddie was becoming toxic from the maggots. Laddie was outside a lot and had diarrhea a few days earlier. That became the target for flies to lay their eggs and develop into maggots.

As I removed more of the fur with the electric clippers, the magnitude of the maggot infestation was becoming more visible. One could now visualize literally hundreds of maggots eating into the flesh of Laddie. Since the clinic was now closed for appointments, Jody's work in the front was finished. So she came to the treatment room to see what we were doing. I had just finished clipping the fur but had not applied the solution to kill the maggots yet. So Jody came in with all the maggots crawling all over poor Laddie. I made a wise crack. "Should we have Rice-A-Roni, the San Francisco treat for lunch today?" Needless to say, the experience did not go over well as Jody ran into the bathroom.

    Fortunately, Laddie recovered well from the shock as we administered fluids and supportive drugs and got rid of the maggots. However, I am not sure that Jody ever recovered from her experience, and to this day, she avoids having Rice-A-Roni, the San Francisco treat.

ABOUT THE AUTHOR

Dr. Douglas Carlson lives in Spring, Texas, with his wife, Paulette. Dr. Doug retired from the veterinary profession after forty-two years of serving the medical and surgical needs of the beloved pets in the Wheaton, Illinois, area. He started the Village Animal Clinic in August 1979 after building a clinic on the northwest side of Wheaton, Illinois. The practice was named one of the best veterinary clinics by the *Chicago* magazine. Currently, his daughter, Dr. Amanda Healey, now owns and operates the clinic and continues to provide excellent service to the needs of pets. Dr. Doug grew up on a pig farm near Red Oak, Iowa, where his experiences with pigs and other animals on the farm contributed to his desire to become a veterinarian.

CPSIA information can be obtained
at www.ICGtesting.com
Printed in the USA
LVHW050458200122
708796LV00008B/577